Easy-to-Follow Vegetarian Instant Pot Cookbook for Beginners:

250 Healthy and Tasty Vegetarian Pressure Cooker Recipes.

by

Noah White

Table of Contents

Introduction

This Vegetarian Instant Pot cookbook is for anyone who is interested in healthy vegetarian cooking. The vegetarian diet is considered as one of the healthiest diets known to man. With the right kitchen appliance, such as the Instant Pot, you will be able to enjoy cooking delicious and healthy food in no time. These recipes are simple with easy-to-follow instructions; whether you are a beginner vegetarian or an old pro, you will love these recipes. Honest vegetarian home cooking doesn't have to be difficult or demand all of your free time. This vegetarian Instant Pot cookbook is the first choice for busy individuals looking for healthy and delicious vegetarian recipes that are insanely simple to prep and cook. This cookbook will be a great help for yourself and your family. Whether you are new to Instant Pot or it is a staple in your kitchen, you will enjoy cooking these vegetarian recipes.

This cookbook includes 250 amazing vegetarian Instant Pot recipes that your family will rave about. Every recipe includes nutritional information so you can easily track exactly what you are consuming. This recipe book includes fresh, whole foods that everyone in the family will enjoy. This vegetarian Instant Pot cookbook will quickly become a go-to resource of inspiration in your kitchen. This cookbook includes a wide variety of ingenious recipes, perfect for any night of the week. This cookbook is your ideal resource for living your best life as a vegetarian. Discover how simple and delicious vegetarian cooking can be with this Instant Pot Cookbook. Scroll to the top and add this amazing vegetarian Instant Pot cookbook to your cart and get your copy today!

Chapter 1 Breakfast

Pear Cinnamon Quinoa

Cook time: 10 minutes |Serves: 4| Per serving: Calories 287; Carbs 39.2g; Fat 12.2g; Protein 7.1g

Ingredients:

- 1 cup Quinoa
- ½ cup of coconut milk
- ½ tsp. baking powder
- ½ tsp. cinnamon
- 1 tsp. vanilla
- 2 tsps. honey
- ½ cup diced pears
- 2 cups water for the pot

Directions:

Mix everything in a bowl. Put 2 cups of water into the Instant Pot or IP and place in the trivet. Place the bowl on the trivet and close the pot. Cook on High for 10 minutes. Open and stir. Serve.

Breakfast Barley

Cook time: 5 minutes |Serves: 4| Per serving: Calories 389; Carbs 49.7g; Fat 19.6g; Protein 8.2g

Ingredients:

- 1 cup barley, rinsed
- 1 cup of coconut milk
- Salt to taste
- ¼ tsp. ground nutmeg
- 1 cup generous mixed berries
- ¼ cup sliced walnuts
- Maple syrup to taste

Directions:

Place the barley in the pot. Add milk, salt, and nutmeg. Cover and cook on High for 5 minutes. Open and fluff the barley with a fork. Top with berries, walnuts, and drizzle with maple syrup. Serve.

Almond Honey Quinoa

Cook time: 5 minutes |Serves: 4 | Per serving: Calories 305; Carbs 53.9g; Fat 8g; Protein 7.7g

Ingredients:

- 1 cup quinoa
- 2 cups of water
- 1 tbsp. coconut oil
- ¼ tsp. salt
- 1 cup almond butter
- 2 cups diced banana
- 2 tbsps. honey
- 1/4 tsp. ground cinnamon

Directions:

Combine water, quinoa, oil, and salt in the pot. Close and cook on High for 5 minutes. Open and stir in butter. Divide quinoa among bowls. Top with banana and drizzle with honey. Sprinkle with cinnamon and serve.

Spinach Muffins

Cook time: 10 minutes |Serves: 2| Per serving: Calories 161; Carbs 2.2g; Fat 12.5g; Protein 10.9g

Ingredients:

- 2 tsps. olive oil, divided
- 1 cup spinach, finely chopped
- ¼ tsp. salt
- 1/8 tsp. black pepper
- 2 large eggs
- 2 tbsps. coconut cream
- 4 tbsps. shredded Parmesan cheese
- 1 cup of water

Directions:

Grease 2 muffin cups with oil. Heat the rest of the oil in the pot. Add spinach, salt, and pepper. Cook for 2 minutes. In a bowl, beat the eggs, cream, and season with salt and pepper. Divide the spinach mixture among 2 muffin cups. Pour the egg mixture over spinach and mix it with a fork. Top with cheese and cover the cups with foil. Pour water into the Instant Pot and place the trivet inside. Place the muffin cups on top. Cover and cook for 5 minutes on High. Serve.

Porridge

Cook time: 15 minutes |Serves: 4| Per serving: Calories 473; Carbs 59.9g; Fat 34.8g; Protein 11.7g

Ingredients:

- 1 cup quinoa

- ¼ cup uncooked buckwheat rinsed and drained
- ¼ cup raisins
- 2 tbsps. ground flax seeds
- 2 tbsps. chia seeds
- 1 tsp. butter
- ¼ tsp. salt
- 1/8 tsp. ground nutmeg
- 2 cups coconut milk plus additional for serving
- 1 ½ cups water
- Honey to taste

Directions:

Combine quinoa, buckwheat, raisins, flax seeds, chia seeds, butter, salt, and nutmeg in a bowl. Mix well. Add milk and blend. Pour water into the pot and place in a rack. Place the bowl on the rack. Cover and cook for 15 minutes on High. Open and stir. Top with raisins and honey and serve.

Honey Nutmeg Cereal Bowls
Cook time: 10 minutes |Serves: 2 | Per serving: Calories 390; Carbs 73.3g; Fat 5.6g; Protein 12.6g

Ingredients:

- 1 cup quinoa
- 1 cup of water
- ½ tsp ground nutmeg
- 1/8 cup honey
- ¼ tsp. vanilla extract
- 1/8 tsp. fine sea salt
- Soy milk for serving
- Chopped fresh fruit of choice

Directions:

Drain and rinse the quinoa. Then combine it with water, nutmeg, honey, vanilla, and salt in the pot. Cover and cook on High for 10 minutes. Open and serve topped with fresh fruit and soy milk.

Mini Frittatas
Cook time: 5 minutes |Serves: 2| Per serving: Calories 242; Carbs 5.8g; Fat 20.9g; Protein 10.3g

Ingredients:

- 3 eggs

- ½ cup of coconut milk
- Salt and pepper to taste
- ¼ cup kale
- ¼ cup chopped broccoli

Directions:

Mix everything in a dish. Pour mixture into silicone molds. Add 1 cup of water in the pot and place in the trivet. Place the silicone molds on top. Cover and cook on High for 5 minutes. Open and serve.

Breakfast Hash

Cook time: 10 minutes |Serves: 4 | Per serving: Calories 344; Carbs 42.7g; Fat 14.4g; Protein 12.3g

Ingredients:

- 2 tbsps. oil
- 4 small sweet potatoes, finely chopped
- 4 eggs
- ½ cup of water
- 2 cups shredded Parmesan cheese

Directions:

Heat the oil in the pot. Brown the sweet potatoes without stirring. Meanwhile, beat the eggs and set aside. Add the water, eggs, cheese in the pot, and mix. Cover and cook for 5 on High minutes. Open and serve.

Omelet Quiche

Cook time: 30 minutes |Serves: 2| Per serving: Calories 112; Carbs 3.3g; Fat 7.4g; Protein 8.5g

Ingredients:

- 2 eggs, beaten
- Salt to taste
- ½ cup milk
- ½ cup jalapeno pepper, diced
- 1 green onion, chopped
- 2 tbsps. cheddar cheese, shredded
- Chopped spring onion tops for serving
- 1 ½ cups water for the pot

Directions:

Add the water in the pot and place the trivet. Grease a baking dish. Set aside. In a bowl, whisk together the milk, eggs, salt, and pepper. Add green onion, jalapenos peppers, and cheese. Mix well. Cover with a foil and place on top of the trivet. Cover the pot and cook on High for 30 minutes. Open and serve with chopped spring onion tops. Serve.

French Toast
Cook time: 25 minutes |Serves: 2| Per serving: Calories 423; Carbs 29.3g; Fat 31.8g; Protein 9.4g

Ingredients:

- 1 cup almond milk
- 1 egg
- 1 tsp. honey
- 1/2 tsp. almond extract
- 1/4 tsp. nutmeg
- 1/8 cup fresh strawberries
- 2 thick slices of French bread cut into 2-inch pieces
- 1 cup water for the pot

Directions:

In a bowl, whisk the eggs, milk, honey, almond extract, and nutmeg until blended. Fold in the strawberry and bread pieces and coat well. Spray baking dish with cooking spray. Pour the bread mixture into the dish. Add the water to the pot and place in a trivet. Add the dish on top of the trivet. Cover and cook for 25 minutes.

Apple Quinoa with Cream
Cook time: 25 minutes |Serves: 2| Per serving: Calories 314; Carbs 55.1g; Fat 31.4g; Protein 8.9g

Ingredients:

- ½ cup quinoa
- 1 cup of water
- 1 cup of coconut milk
- 1/8 tsp. salt
- 1/8 tsp. ground nutmeg
- 2 tbsps. maple syrup
- ½ cup apple, chopped
- Maple syrup, milk, and cream for serving

Directions:

Add everything in the Instant Pot and cover. Cook on Multigrain for 6 minutes. Open and serve with maple syrup, milk, and cream.

Breakfast Cobbler

Cook time:25 minutes |Serves: 4| Per serving: Calories 284; Carbs 47.2g; Fat 12.3g; Protein 2.3g

Ingredients:

- 2 peaches, diced
- 2 apples, diced
- 1 cup blueberries
- 4 tbsps. honey
- 2 tbsps. oil
- ½ tsp. nutmeg
- ½ cup shredded coconut, unsweetened
- 4 tbsps. sunflower seeds
- Cream for serving

Directions:

Place the fruits into the pot. Add honey, oil, and nutmeg. Cover and press Steam. Cook for 10 minutes. Then open and remove the cooked fruit. Now add the coconut, and seeds into the residual liquid and press Sauté. Cook and stir for 5 minutes. Serve topped with cream.

Swiss Chard Muffins

Cook time: 10 minutes |Serves: 2| Per serving: Calories 166; Carbs 1g; Fat 4.7g; Protein 5.1g

Ingredients:

- 2 eggs
- 1/8 tsp. pepper seasoning
- 4 tbsps. shredded goat's cheese
- 1 green onion, diced
- ½ cup Swiss chard, chopped
- 1 ½ cups of water

Directions:

Add the water in the Instant Pot and place in a trivet. Break the eggs in a bowl. Season and beat well. Divide the cheese, chard, and green onion between muffin cups. Pour the beaten eggs into each muffin cup and mix. Place the muffin cups on the trivet. Cover and cook on High for 8 minutes. Open and remove. Serve.

Scrambled Eggs with Cheese

Cook time: 10 minutes |Serves: 4| Per serving: Calories 342; Carbs 1.9g; Fat 31g; Protein 15.7g

Ingredients:

- 8 eggs

- 2 cups of goat's cheese, grated
- 4 tbsps. coconut oil
- Salt and pepper to taste
- 4 tbsps. coconut milk
- 1 cup of water for the pot

Directions:

Grease a bowl with cooking spray and break eggs in the bowl. Add milk, salt, and pepper and beat. Add the cheese and mix. Add 1 cup water to the pot and place in a trivet. Cover and cook on Steam for 7 minutes at Low. Open and serve.

Vegetable Muffins
Cook time: 6 minutes |Serves: 2| Per serving: Calories 162; Carbs 5.4g; Fat 10.1g; Protein 13.1g

Ingredients:

- 1/2 bell pepper, red
- 1 spring onion, chopped
- 4 eggs
- 1/2 handful kale
- 1/4 cup goat's cheese
- ¼ tsp. salt
- 1 tsp. hot sauce
- 1 cup water for the pot

Directions:

Grease 2 custard cups with cooking spray. In a bowl, whisk the eggs, salt, cheese, and pepper. Evenly divide the kale, bell pepper, and spring onion among the custard cups. Pour the egg mixture over the veggies. Pour 1 cup water into the Instant Pot and place in a trivet. Cover and cook on High for 6 minutes. Do a quick release and open. Serve.

Quinoa Breakfast Muffins
Cook time: 5 minutes |Serves: 2| Per serving: Calories 339; Carbs 59g; Fat 12.7g; Protein 23g

Ingredients:

- 1 cup cooked quinoa
- 2 eggs
- 1/2 cup chopped fresh spinach leaves
- 1 /2 cup cherry tomatoes
- 1/2 cup sliced mushrooms
- 1/2 cup cubed zucchini
- ½ cup grated parmesan cheese

- Salt and pepper to taste
- Coconut oil to brush the tins
- 1 cup water for the pot

Directions:

Grease custard cups with cooking spray. In a bowl, whisk the eggs, cheese, salt, and pepper. Divide the quinoa, spinach, tomatoes, mushrooms, and zucchini among the cups. Pour the egg mixture over the veggies. Pour 1 cup water into the Instant Pot and place in a trivet. Place the cups on the top of the trivet. Cover the pot and cook for 6 minutes on High. Do a quick release and open. Serve.

Buckwheat Porridge
Cook time: 6 minutes |Serves: 4| Per serving: Calories 205; Carbs 35g; Fat 3g; Protein 8g

Ingredients:

- 1 cup buckwheat groats (raw)
- 3 cups of rice milk
- 1 sliced banana
- 1/4 cup raisins
- 1 tbsp cinnamon
- 1/2 tbsp vanilla essence

Directions:

Place the buckwheat, banana, cinnamon, milk, raisins, and vanilla in the pot. Cover and cook on High for 6 minutes. Do a quick release and open. Serve.

Strawberries and Oats
Cook time: 10 minutes |Serves: 2| Per serving: Calories 200; Carbs 25g; Fat 5g; Protein 8.6g

Ingredients:

- 1/2 cup rolled oats (old-fashioned)
- 2 tbsps. strawberries (dried)
- 1 cup almond milk
- 1/2 tbsp coconut sugar
- Salt to taste
- 1 cup of water

Directions:

Add water, milk, oats, sugar, and strawberries to the pot. Cover and cook for 10 minutes on High. Do a quick release and open. Divide among bowls and sprinkle with salt. Serve.

Banana Nut Oatmeal
Cook time: 18 minutes |Serves: 3| Per serving: Calories 205; Carbs 35g; Fat 3g; Protein 8g

Ingredients:

- 1 cup steel-cut oats
- 2 sliced bananas
- 1 tbsp cinnamon
- 1/2 cup sliced almonds
- Maple syrup, to taste
- 3 cups of water

Directions:

Place 1 banana, 3 cups water, oats, and cinnamon in the pot and mix. Cover and cook on High for 18 minutes. Open and serve between 3 bowls. Add sliced banana, maple syrup, and almond slices. Serve.

Apple Cinnamon Steel Cut Oats
Cook time: 4 minutes |Serves: 2| Per serving: Calories 350; Carbs 62g; Fat 7g; Protein 13g

Ingredients:

- 2 cups steel-cut oats
- 2 cups of water
- 2 medium apples, diced
- 2 tsps brown sugar
- 2 tsps. cinnamon
- ¼ tsp nutmeg
- More cinnamon and sliced apples for serving

Directions:

Place everything in the pot and mix. Cover and cook on High for 4 minutes. Open and stir. Top with additional cinnamon and diced apples. Serve.

Instant Pot Barley
Cook time: 24 minutes |Serves: 4| Per serving: Calories 217; Carbs 15g; Fat 10g; Protein 14g

Ingredients:

- 1 tbsp olive oil
- 1 cup pearl barley
- 1/3 cup red or sweet onion, finely chopped
- 4 cups liquid, half broth (vegetable) and half water
- Sea salt to taste
- 4 oz baby greens
- 4 eggs, half boiled

Directions:

Heat the oil in the Instant Pot. Add barley and onion and cook for 5 minutes. Add the liquid and salt. Cover and cook on High for 18 minutes. Do a quick release and open. Drain the mix and remove to serving bowls. Add the baby greens to the pot and cook for 1 minute. Serve barley mixture with egg and baby greens.

Mexican Breakfast Casserole
Cook time: 15 minutes |Serves: 4| Per serving: Calories 356; Carbs 29g; Fat 8g; Protein 18g

Ingredients:

- 2 tbsps olive oil (1 to grease the baking dish)
- ½ cup diced yellow onion
- ½ cup diced red bell pepper
- 1 clove garlic, minced
- 2 medium sweet potatoes, peeled and shredded
- 5 eggs
- ½ tsp chili powder
- 1 cup of water
- Salt and pepper to taste
- Parsley leaves, chopped

Directions:

Heat the oil on Sauté. Add the onion, sweet potatoes, pepper, garlic, and cook for 3 minutes. Remove the mix to a greased casserole dish. Whisk salt, eggs, pepper, and chili powder in a bowl and pour over the potato mixture. Clean the pot and add water to the pot. Place in a trivet and place the casserole dish on top of the trivet. Cover and cook on High for 12 minutes. Do a quick release and open. Sprinkle with parsley and serve.

Sweet Potatoes with Poached Eggs
Cook time: 15 minutes |Serves: 4 | Per serving: Calories 313; Carbs 25 g; Fat 19g; Protein 13g

Ingredients:

- 4 sweet potatoes, peeled (5 oz each)
- 1 cup of water
- 8 eggs, poached
- 2 avocados
- Fresh coriander leaves to taste
- Salt and pepper to taste

Directions:

Add 1 cup water to the pot and place the trivet. Place the potatoes on the trivet. Cover and cook on High for 15 minutes. Do a quick release and open. Cut potatoes in half and place an egg on each half. Season with salt and pepper. Serve with avocado and coriander leaves.

Quinoa Blueberry Breakfast Bowl
Cook time: 5 minutes |Serves: 4| Per serving: Calories 300; Carbs 48g; Fat 9g; Protein 13g

Ingredients:

- 1½ cups white quinoa
- 1½ cups water
- 1 cinnamon stick
- ¼ cup raisins
- 1 tbsp. honey plus more for serving
- 1 cup apple juice
- ¾ cup apple, grated
- 1½ cups plain yogurt
- ¼ cup pistachios, chopped
- Blueberries to serve

Directions:

Rinse the quinoa. Add water, quinoa, and cinnamon to the Instant Pot. Cover and cook on High for 5 minutes. Open and pour the quinoa into serving bowls. Remove the cinnamon stick and add raisins, honey, apple, apple juice, and mix. Refrigerate for 1 hour, add the yogurt and mix. Serve topped with yogurt, honey, pistachios, and blueberries.

Brown Rice Congee with Mushrooms and Bok Choy
Cook time: 22 minutes |Serves: 3| Per serving: Calories 400; Carbs 68g; Fat 8g; Protein 15g

Ingredients:

- ½ cup of brown rice
- 4 cups mushroom broth
- 2 cups bok choy, chopped
- 2 cups mushrooms, sliced in half lengthwise
- 2 tbsps. fresh ginger, minced
- 2 cloves garlic, minced
- ½ cup scallions, diced
- 1 block (14 oz) cooked tofu
- Soy sauce to taste

Directions:

Combine everything except the tofu and scallions in the pot. Cover and cook on High for 22 minutes. Do a quick release and open. Add the cooked tofu and scallions. Add soy sauce to taste and serve.

Sweet Corn Porridge
Cook time: 2 minutes |Serves: 4| Per serving: Calories 311; Carbs 38.9g; Fat 15.8g; Protein 3.4g

Ingredients:

- 1 cup yellow cornmeal, coarse
- 4 cups of water
- ¼ cup of coconut milk
- 2 tbsps. coconut sugar
- ¼ tsp cinnamon powder
- ½ tsp vanilla extract
- ¼ tsp nutmeg powder
- 4 tbsps. butter
- Sliced papaya, raspberries, and toasted shredded coconut as toppings

Directions:

Add cornmeal, water, milk, sugar, cinnamon powder, vanilla, and nutmeg in the pot. Mix and close the pot. Cook on High for 2 minutes. Do a quick release and open. Add the butter and mix until butter melts. Top with toppings and serve.

Cranberry Rice Pudding
Cook time: 5 minutes |Serves: 4| Per serving: Calories 381; Carbs 76g; Fat 3g; Protein 11.5g

Ingredients:

- 1 cup jasmine rice, rinsed
- 4 cups of coconut milk
- ½ tsp nutmeg powder
- 1 tsp vanilla extract
- ¼ cup maple syrup
- ½ cup dried cranberries
- ¼ cup almond

Directions:

Add the rice, milk, nutmeg, vanilla extract, and maple syrup in the pot. Close and cook on High for 5 minutes. Open and add cranberries and stir. Serve topped with almonds.

Maple Kiwi Oatmeal
Cook time: 3 minutes |Serves: 4| Per serving: Calories 443; Carbs 74g; Fat 8g; Protein 20g

Ingredients:

- 2 cups Scottish oatmeal
- 8 cups almond milk
- ½ cup maple syrup
- 2 tbsps. butter
- 1 tsp vanilla extract
- ½ tsp salt
- ½ tsp cinnamon powder
- ½ tsp nutmeg powder
- Chopped mangos, chopped kiwis, toasted coconut shavings, and cinnamon as toppings

Directions:

Add oats, milk, syrup, butter, vanilla, salt, cinnamon, and nutmeg in the pot. Mix and close. Cook on High for 3 minutes. Do a quick release and open. Stir and adjust taste with some more syrup. Top with toppings and serve.

Raspberry Toast Casserole
Cook time: 15 minutes |Serves: 4| Per serving: Calories 287; Carbs 25.8g; Fat 11.2g; Protein 6.9g

Ingredients:

- 1 loaf multigrain bread, chopped
- 1 cup milk
- 1 tbsp brown sugar
- 2 tbsps. cornstarch
- 1 tsp vanilla extract
- 2 tbsps. melted butter
- A pinch salt
- ¼ tsp cinnamon powder
- ¼ cup raspberries
- 1 cup water for the pot
- Maple syrup for serving

Directions:

In a bowl, whisk the milk, sugar, cornstarch, vanilla, butter, salt, and cinnamon. Add the water to the pot and place a trivet. In a bowl, add the bread slices and raspberries and pour the cornstarch mixture. Cover the bowl with foil and place the bowl on the trivet. Close and cook on High for 15 minutes. Do a quick release and open. Drizzle with some maple syrup and serve.

Tropical Fruits Grits
Cook time: 10 minutes |Serves: 4| Per serving: Calories 336; Carbs 75g; Fat 1.7g; Protein 5.3g

Ingredients:

- 1 ½ cups yellow cornmeal grits
- 2 cups of water
- ¾ cup milk + extra for topping
- ½ tsp salt
- 2 tbsps. maple syrup + extra for topping

For topping

- 2 kiwis, peeled and chopped
- ¼ cup chopped pineapples
- 2 bananas, sliced
- 4 strawberries, sliced

Directions:

Add the water, cornmeal grits, milk, salt, and maple syrup in the pot. Mix. Close and cook for 10 minutes on High. Open and add milk on top. Then add the toppings. Serve.

Carrot and Pineapple Muffins
Cook time: 8 minutes |Serves: 4| Per serving: Calories 442; Carbs 74g; Fat 36.7g; Protein 5.3g

Ingredients:

- 2 tbsp. flaxseed meal + 6 tbsp. water
- 2/3 cup oil
- 1 tsp vanilla extract
- 1 cup of sugar
- 1 ½ cups plain flour
- 1 tsp baking soda
- 1 tsp cinnamon powder
- ¼ tsp salt
- 2 tsps. baking powder
- 1 cup chopped pineapple, crushed
- 1 cup grated carrots
- 2 cups of water

Directions:

In a bowl, whisk the flaxseed meal and water and set aside for 15 minutes. Then whisk in the oil and vanilla. In another bowl, combine flour, sugar, baking soda, cinnamon, salt, and baking powder. Mix well. Fold in carrots and pineapples. Spoon the mixture into 12-holed silicone egg mold. Add the water to the pot and place in a trivet. Place the egg molds on top. Cover the egg molds with foil. Close the lid and cook on High for 8 minutes. Do a quick release and open. Cool and serve.

Sunday Brunch Broccoli Egg Cups
Cook time: 6 minutes |Serves: 4| Per serving: Calories 274; Carbs 5g; Fat 19g; Protein 16g

Ingredients:

- 7 eggs
- 1 1/2 cups half-and-half cream
- 3 tbsps. shredded Swiss cheese
- 2 tsps. minced parsley
- 1 tsp. minced fresh basil
- 1/4 tsp. salt
- 1/8 tsp. cayenne pepper
- 1 1/2 cups broccoli florets
- 1 cup of water

Directions:

Whisk three eggs with the next six ingredients. Pour into 4 greased ramekins. Divide broccoli among ramekins. Then top each with one remaining egg. Add 1 cup water to the pot and place a trivet. Place the ramekins on the trivet and cover with the foil. Close the pot and cook on High for 6 minutes. Do a quick release. Open and serve.

Omelet Frittata
Cook time: 35 minutes |Serves: 6| Per serving: Calories 320; Carbs 12g; Fat 19g; Protein 15g

Ingredients:

- 1 tbsp. olive oil
- 1 medium potato, peeled and sliced
- 1 small onion, thinly sliced
- 1 cup of water
- 12 large eggs
- 1 tsp. hot pepper sauce
- 1/2 tsp. salt
- 1/4 tsp. pepper
- 1/2 cup chopped green pepper
- 1 cup shredded cheddar cheese, divided

Directions:

Add oil and heat on Sauté. Add onion, potato, and cook for 5 minutes. Transfer to a baking dish. Clean the pot and add water and a trivet. In a bowl, whisk eggs, pepper sauce, salt, and pepper.

Add green pepper and ½ cup cheese. Pour over potato mixture and top with remaining cheese. Cover the baking dish with foil and place it on the trivet. Cover the pot and cook on High for 35 minutes. Open and serve.

Frittata Provencal
Cook time: 40 minutes |Serves: 6| Per serving: Calories 245; Carbs 12g; Fat 14g; Protein 15g

Ingredients:

- 1 tbsp. olive oil
- 1 medium potato, peeled and sliced
- 1 small onion, thinly sliced
- 1/2 tsp. smoked paprika
- 1 cup of water
- 12 eggs
- 1 tsp. minced fresh thyme
- 1 tsp. hot pepper sauce
- 1/2 tsp. salt
- 1/4 tsp. pepper
- 4 oz. crumbled fresh goat's cheese, divided
- 1/2 cup chopped sun-dried tomatoes (not packed in oil)

Directions:

Heat the oil on Sauté. Add onion and potato and cook for 5 to 7 minutes. Stir in paprika. Transfer potato mixture to a baking dish. Clean the pot. Add water and a trivet. In a bowl, whisk the eggs, thyme, sauce, salt, and pepper. Stir in 2 oz. cheese. Pour over the potato mixture. Top with remaining cheese and tomatoes. Cover the dish with foil and place it on a trivet. Cover the pot and cook on High for 35 minutes. Open, slice, and serve.

Potato-Cheddar Frittata
Cook time: 30 minutes |Serves: 4| Per serving: Calories 241; Carbs 11g; Fat 13g; Protein 19g

Ingredients:

- 1 tbsp. oil
- 1 1/2 cups diced potatoes
- ¼ cup chopped onion
- 1 cup of water
- 8 egg whites
- 4 eggs
- 1/2 cup milk
- 2 green onions, chopped
- 2 tsps. minced fresh parsley

- 1/4 tsp. salt
- 1/4 tsp. pepper
- 1/2 cup shredded cheddar cheese

Directions:

Heat oil in the pot on Sauté. Add potatoes and cook for 5 minutes. Transfer to a greased baking dish. Clean the pot and add 1 cup water and a trivet in the pot. Whisk the next seven ingredients (starting with egg whites) and stir in cheese. Pour egg mixture over potatoes. Loosely cover the baking dish with foil and place over the trivet. Cover the pot and cook on High for 30 minutes. Do a quick release and open. Serve.

Carrot Cake Oatmeal

Cook time: 10 minutes |Serves: 8 | Per serving: Calories 197; Carbs 46g; Fat 2g; Protein 4g

Ingredients:

- 4 1/2 cups water
- 1 can (20 oz.) crushed pineapple, undrained
- 2 cups shredded carrots
- 1 cup steel-cut oats
- 1 cup raisins
- 2 tsps. ground cinnamon
- 1 tsp. pumpkin pie spice
- Brown sugar

Directions:

Coat the inside the pot with cooking spray. Combine the first seven ingredients and mix. Cover and cook on High for 10 minutes. Do a quick release and open. Sprinkle with brown sugar and serve.

Chapter 2 Snacks and Appetizers

Zesty Eggs
Cook time: 8 minutes |Serves: 4| Per serving: Calories 88; Carbs 2g; Fat 6.3g; Protein 5.8g

Ingredients:

- 4 eggs
- 1½ tbsps. Greek yogurt
- 1½ tbsps. mayonnaise
- ½ tsp. jalapeno, chopped
- ¼ tsp. onion powder
- ¼ tsp. paprika
- ¼ tsp. lemon zests
- Salt and black pepper, to taste
- 1 cup water for the pot

Directions:

Place the trivet in the pot and add 1 cup of water. Place the eggs on the trivet and cover the pot. Cook on High for 6 minutes. Open and place the eggs into ice-cold water. Peel the eggs, and cut in half, lengthwise. Scoop out the egg yolks and mix them with the rest of the ingredients. Fill the hollow eggs with this mixture and serve.

Egg Zucchini
Cook time: 5 minutes |Serves: 2| Per serving: Calories 134; Carbs 8g; Fat 10g; Protein 5.1g

Ingredients:

- 1 zucchini, cut into ½ inch round slices
- ½ tsp. dried dill
- ½ tsp. paprika
- 1 egg
- 1 tbsp. coconut oil
- 1½ tbsps. coconut flour
- 1 tbsp. milk
- Salt and black pepper, to taste

Directions:

Whisk egg and milk in a bowl. Mix the salt, black pepper, paprika, dried dill, and flour in another bowl. Dip the zucchini slices in the egg mixture then in the dry mixture. Heat the oil in the pot and add the zucchini slices. Cook on Sauté for 5 minutes. Serve.

Egg Veggie Mix

Cook time: 10 minutes |Serves: 8| Per serving: Calories 192; Carbs 16.2g; Fat 8.9g; Protein 12.3g

Ingredients:

- 16 eggs, beaten
- 2 sweet potatoes, peeled and shredded
- 2 red bell peppers, seeded and chopped
- 2 onions, chopped
- 2 garlic cloves, minced
- 4 tsps. fresh basil, chopped
- Salt and black pepper, to taste
- 2 tbsps. oil

Directions:

Put everything in the pot and mix well. Cover and cook on High for 8 minutes. Open and serve.

Turmeric Egg Potatoes

Cook time: 10 minutes |Serves: 3| Per serving: Calories 265; Carbs 28.1g; Fat 14.7g; Protein 6.9g

Ingredients:

- 2 eggs, whisked
- 1 tsp. ground turmeric
- 1 tsp. cumin seeds
- 2 tbsps. olive oil
- 2 potatoes, peeled and diced
- 1 onion, finely chopped
- 2 tsps. ginger-garlic paste
- ½ tsp. red chili powder
- Salt and black pepper, to taste

Directions:

Add oil, cumin seed, ginger-garlic paste, and onions in the pot and cook on Sauté for 4 minutes. Add the rest of the ingredients and cover. Cook on High for 6 minutes. Open and serve.

Sauté Nuts

Cook time: 20 minutes |Serves: 6| Per serving: Calories 335; Carbs 31.5g; Fat 22.4g; Protein 8.1g

Ingredients:

- 1 cup cashews
- 1 cup almonds
- 1 cup pecans

- 1 cup raisins
- 1 tbsp. butter
- ½ tsp. brown sugar
- ½ tsp. black pepper
- 1½ tsp. chili powder
- ½ tsp. sea salt
- ½ tsp. garlic powder
- ¼ tsp. cayenne pepper
- ½ tsp. cumin powder

Directions:

Put the butter, almonds, cashews, raisins, and pecans in the pot. Season with all the spices and mix. Cover and cook on High for 20 minutes.

Mushroom Spinach Treat

Cook time: 12 minutes |Serves: 3| Per serving: Calories 86; Carbs 8.1g; Fat 5.32g; Protein 4g

Ingredients:

- ½ cup spinach
- ½ pound fresh mushrooms, sliced
- 2 garlic cloves, minced
- 2 tbsps. fresh thyme, chopped
- 1 onion, chopped
- 1 tbsp. olive oil
- 1 tbsp. fresh cilantro, chopped, for garnish
- Salt and black pepper, to taste

Directions:

Put the oil, garlic, and onions in the pot and press Sauté. Sauté for 4 minutes and add the rest of the ingredients. Mix and cover. Cook on High for 7 minutes. Open and garnish with cilantro. Serve.

Spicy Roasted Olives

Cook time: 7 minutes |Serves: 4| Per serving: Calories 163; Carbs 2.3g; Fat 13.6g; Protein 0.4g

Ingredients:

- 2 cups green and black olives, mixed
- 2 tangerines
- 2 garlic cloves, minced
- 2 tbsps. vinegar
- ½ inch piece of turmeric, finely grated
- 1 fresh red chili, thinly sliced

- 2 sprigs rosemary
- 1 tbsp. olive oil

Directions:

Put all the ingredients except the tangerines in the pot. Squeeze the tangerines in the pot over the other ingredients. Cover and cook on High for 6 minutes. Open and serve.

Cooked Guacamole
Cook time: 10 minutes |Serves: 4| Per serving: Calories 401; Carbs 19.4g; Fat 37.4g; Protein 4.1g

Ingredients:

- 1 large onion, finely diced
- 4 tbsps. lemon juice
- ¼ cup cilantro, chopped
- 4 avocados, peeled and diced
- 3 tbsps. olive oil
- 3 jalapenos, finely diced
- Salt and black pepper, to taste

Directions:

Heat the oil on Sauté. Add onions and cook for 3 minutes. Add the rest of the ingredients and mix. Cover and cook on High for 6 minutes. Serve.

Butternut Squash
Cook time: 7 minutes |Serves: 2| Per serving: Calories 154; Carbs 19.5g; Fat 6.6g; Protein 3.1

Ingredients:

- 1 whole butternut squash, washed
- 1 tbsp. butter
- 1 tbsp. BBQ sauce
- Salt and black pepper, to taste
- ¼ tsp. smoked paprika

Directions:

Season the squash with paprika, salt, and pepper. Put the butter and seasoned squash in the pot. Cover and cook on High for 6 minutes. Open and top with BBQ sauce. Serve.

Cajun Spiced Pecans
Cook time: 20 minutes |Serves: 3| Per serving: Calories 345; Carbs 7.2g; Fat 33.1g; Protein 4.4g

Ingredients:

- ½ pound pecan halves

- 1 tsp. dried basil
- 1 tsp. dried thyme
- ½ tbsp. chili powder
- ¼ tsp. garlic powder
- ¼ tsp. cayenne pepper
- 1 tbsp. olive oil
- 1 tsp. dried oregano
- Salt, to taste

Directions:

Put everything in the pot. Cover and cook on Low for 20 minutes. Open and serve.

Energy Booster Cookies

Cook time: 10 minutes |Serves: 6| Per serving: Calories 107; Carbs 17.1g; Fat 4.8g; Protein 4.5g

Ingredients:

- 2 eggs
- 2/3 cup cocoa powder
- 1/3 cup sugar
- 1 ¼ cups butter
- Salt to taste
- 1 cup water for the pot

Directions:

Put everything in a food processor and pulse. Roll the mixture into 12 equal balls and press them. Arrange the balls onto a lined cookie sheet. Place a trivet in the pot and add water. Place the cookie sheet on the trivet. Cover the pot and cook on High for 10 minutes. Open and serve.

Cooked Peaches

Cook time: 7 minutes |Serves: 5| Per serving: Calories 109; Carbs 14.6g; Fat 6g; Protein 1.4g

Ingredients:

- 5 medium peaches, pits removed
- ¼ tsp. ground cloves
- ½ tsp. ground cinnamon
- ½ tsp. brown sugar
- 2 tbsps. olive oil
- ¼ tsp. salt
- 1 cup water for the pot

Directions:

Add oil on the cut side of the peaches. Sprinkle the peaches with salt, cloves, cinnamon, and brown sugar. Place the trivet in the pot and add water. Place the peaches on it. Cover and cook on High for 7 minutes. Open and serve.

Honey Citrus Roasted Cashews
Cook time: 25 minutes |Serves: 2| Per serving: Calories 292; Carbs 43g; Fat 12.3g; Protein 5.2g

Ingredients:

- ¾ cup cashews
- ¼ tsp. salt
- ¼ tsp. ginger powder
- 1 tsp. orange zest, minced
- 4 tbsps. honey
- 1 cup water for the pot

Directions:

Mix together honey, orange zest, ginger powder, and salt. Add cashews to this mixture and place it in a ramekin. Place a trivet in the pot and add water. Place the ramekin on the trivet and close the pot. Cook on High for 20 minutes. Open and serve.

Pumpkin Muffins
Cook time: 15 minutes |Serves: 10 | Per serving: Calories 268; Carbs 25.7g; Fat 15.9g; Protein 8.7g

Ingredients:

- 2 cups almond flour
- 4 tbsps. coconut flour
- 1½ tsps. baking soda
- 2 tsps. pumpkin pie spice
- ¼ tsp. salt
- 1 cup pumpkin puree
- 3 tsps. butter
- 1½ tsps. baking powder
- ½ tsp. ground cinnamon
- 3 large eggs
- ½ cup raw honey
- 2 tbsps. almonds, toasted and chopped
- 1 cup water for the pot

Directions:

In a bowl, whisk together almond flour, coconut flour, cinnamon, baking soda, baking powder, salt, and pumpkin pie spice. Whisk together eggs, honey, pumpkin puree, and butter. Combine both mixtures. Fill a greased muffin pan and top with almonds. Place a trivet in the pot and add water. Place the muffin pan on top of the trivet. Cover the pot and cook on High for 12 minutes. Open and serve.

Banana Chips
Cook time: 25 minutes |Serves: 3| Per serving: Calories 145; Carbs 30.7g; Fat 3.1g; Protein 1.8g

Ingredients:

- 3 bananas, cut into 1/8-inch slices
- 3 tbsps. lemon juice
- 3 tbsps. nutmeg
- 1 cup water for the pot

Directions:

Mix everything in a bowl. Spread banana slices on a baking sheet. Place the trivet in the pot and add water. Place the baking sheet on it. Cook on High for 25 minutes. Open and serve.

Mustard Flavored Artichokes
Cook time: 12 minutes |Serves: 3| Per serving: Calories 147; Carbs 24.4g; Fat 5.4g; Protein 6g

Ingredients:

- 3 artichokes
- 3 tbsps. mayonnaise
- 1 cup water for the pot
- 2 pinches paprika
- 2 lemons, sliced in half
- 2 tsps. Dijon mustard

Directions:

Mix mayonnaise, paprika, and mustard. Place the trivet in the pot and add water. Place the artichokes upwards and arrange the lemon slices on it. Cover the pot and cook on High for 12 minutes. Open and put the artichokes in the mayonnaise mixture. Serve.

Queso Blanco
Cook time: 10 minutes |Serves: 10| Per serving: Calories 153; Carbs 2.5g; Fat 13g; Protein 6.6g

Ingredients:

- ½ (8-ounce) package Neufchatel cheese
- 1 can of minced green chili
- 8 ounces of shredded Oaxaca cheese
- 4 ounces heavy cream
- 1 tbsp. minced pickled jalapeno pepper

- 1 ½ tsps. pickled jalapeno pepper juice

Directions:

Add Neufchatel cheese, Oaxaca cheese, heavy cream, and cook on Sauté until melted. Cook for 5 minutes and mix well. Add jalapeno peppers, green chili, and juice. Mix and serve.

Smoky Pecan Brussels Sprouts
Cook time: 8 minutes |Serves: 2| Per serving: Calories 113; Carbs 17g; Fat 3g; Protein 5g

Ingredients:

- 2 cups small baby Brussels sprouts
- ¼ cup of water
- ½ tsp liquid smoke
- ¼ cup pecans, chopped
- 2 tbsps. maple syrup
- Salt and pepper to taste

Directions:

Add water, Brussels sprouts, and liquid smoke to the Instant Pot. Mix well and cover. Cook on High for 2 minutes. Open and press Sauté. Add pecans, maple syrup, and cook until liquid is reduced, about 5 to 7 minutes. Season with salt and pepper and serve.

Honey Soy Carrots
Cook time: 6 minutes |Serves: 4| Per serving: Calories 80; Carbs 18g; Fat 0g; Protein 5g

Ingredients:

- 8 medium-size carrots
- 1 cup of water
- 1 clove garlic, finely chopped
- 1 tbsp honey
- 2 tbsps. soy sauce
- ½ tbsp sesame seeds
- Salt to taste
- Green onions, chopped, for garnish

Directions:

Add carrots and water to the Instant Pot. Cover and cook on High for 3 minutes. Open and remove the carrots. Drain the water. Press Sauté and add the remaining ingredients except for the green onions and sesame seeds. Cook until sticky. Put carrots back into the pot and coat well. Sprinkle with green onions and seeds and serve.

Carrots in Thyme

Cook time: 5 minutes |Serves: 2| Per serving: Calories 77; Carbs 6g; Fat 5.8g; Protein 1g

Ingredients:

- 4 carrots, peeled
- 1½ tsp. fresh thyme
- 2 tbsps. butter
- ½ cup of water
- 1 dash salt

Directions:

Melt the butter on Sauté. Cut the peeled carrots like French fries. Add carrots, thyme, salt, and ½ cup water to the pot. Cover and cook for 2 minutes. Open and serve.

Spicy Cauliflower

Cook time: 10 minutes |Serves: 4| Per serving: Calories 305; Carbs 54g; Fat 7g; Protein 14g

Ingredients:

- 1 large cauliflower, cleaned and cut into florets
- 2 tbsps. olive oil
- 1 large onion, finely chopped
- ½ tsp ginger powder
- 1 cup of water
- 4 tbsps. cilantro, chopped
- ½ tsp turmeric powder
- 1 tbsp coriander powder
- 1 tbsp cumin powder
- ½ tsp garam masala
- ½ tsp chili powder

Directions:

Heat oil on Sauté. Add oil and cook for 30 seconds. Add onion and sauté for 4 minutes. Add remaining spices and cook for 30 seconds. Add cauliflower florets and cook for 1 minute. Add water and cover. Cook on High for 3 minutes. Do a quick release and open. Add cilantro and mix. Serve.

Creamy Garlic Broccoli Mash

Cook time: 4 minutes |Serves: 4| Per serving: Calories 166; Carbs 7g; Fat 13g; Protein 5g

Ingredients:

- 1 tbsp olive oil
- 3 medium cloves garlic, crushed

- 2 medium heads broccoli. chopped
- ½ cup of water
- 4 oz cream cheese
- ¼ tsp red pepper flakes, crushed
- Salt and pepper to taste

Directions:

Heat oil on Sauté. Add garlic and cook for 30 seconds. Add remaining ingredients and cook on High for 2 minutes. Open and mash the broccoli with a blender. Season and serve.

Polenta
Cook time: 15 minutes |Serves: 6| Per serving: Calories 170; Carbs 22g; Fat 6g; Protein 5g

Ingredients:

- 1 cup polenta (coarse-ground cornmeal)
- 4 cups vegetable broth
- 4 tsps. butter
- ½ cup Mexican blend shredded cheese
- ¼ cup half and half
- Salt to taste

Directions:

Bring the broth and polenta to a boil on Sauté. Once it starts to boil, cover, and cook on High for 7 minutes. Open and blend in the butter, cheese, and half and half. Add salt and serve.

Spicy Creamed Corn
Cook time: 6 minutes |Serves: 4| Per serving: Calories 376; Carbs 26g; Fat 30g; Protein 6g

Ingredients:

- 32 oz corn kernels
- 8 oz cream cheese, cubed
- ½ cup butter, cubed
- ½ cup milk
- ½ cup heavy cream
- 1 tsp cayenne pepper
- ½ tsp black pepper
- 1 tbsp sugar
- 1 tsp salt

Directions:

Add everything in the pot and mix. Cover and cook on Low for 6 minutes. Open and serve.

Mushroom Pate

Cook time: 17 minutes |Serves: 6| Per serving: Calories 86; Carbs 4.6g; Fat 6.5g; Protein 3g

Ingredients:

- ¾ cup porcini mushrooms, dry
- 1 pound crèmini mushrooms, sliced
- 1 tbsp. margarine
- 1 cup hot water
- 1 shallot, sliced
- 2 tbsps. olive oil
- Salt and white pepper to the taste
- ¼ cup white wine
- 3 tbsps. cheese, grated
- 1 bay leaf
- Toasted bread slices for serving

Directions:

Put dry mushrooms in a bowl and add water. Cover and set aside. Press Sauté on the pot. Add margarine and 1 tbsp. oil. Add shallot and cook for 2 minutes. Add fresh mushrooms and cook for 5 minutes. Add wine and rehydrated mushrooms, salt, pepper, and bay leaf. Mix and cover. Cook on High for 10 minutes. Open and discard bay leaf. Add the rest of the oil, cheese, and pulse with a hand mixer until smooth. Serve with toasted bread slices.

Olive, Eggplant Spread

Cook time: 8 minutes |Serves: 6| Per serving: Calories 155; Carbs 14g; Fat 11g; Protein 2g

Ingredients:

- 2 pounds eggplant, sliced
- A pinch of salt and black pepper
- 4 tbsps. olive oil
- 4 garlic cloves, chopped
- ½ cup of water
- Juice of 1 lemon
- ¼ cup black olives, pitted
- 1 tbsp. sesame paste
- 4 thyme sprigs, chopped

Directions:

Heat oil on Sauté. Add eggplant and cook for 5 minutes. Add water, salt, and pepper. Mix and cover. Cook on High for 3 minutes. Add the remaining ingredients and mix with a hand mixer. Serve.

Artichoke Dip

Cook time: 20 minutes |Serves: 6| Per serving: Calories 210; Carbs 8g; Fat 2g; Protein 8g

Ingredients:

- ½ cup cannellini beans, soaked for 12 hours and drained
- 2 garlic cloves, minced
- Juice of ½ lemon
- 1 cup of water
- 1-pound baby artichokes, trimmed and stems cut off
- 1 cup cream
- A pinch of salt and black pepper

Directions:

In the pot, mix beans, artichokes, water, salt, and pepper. Mix and cover. Cook on High for 20 minutes. Add garlic and cream. Blend with a hand mixer. Serve.

Caramelized Garlic

Cook time: 6 minutes |Serves: 3 | Per serving: Calories 152; Carbs 6g; Fat 4g; Protein 8g

Ingredients:

- 3 big garlic heads, tops cut off
- 1 cup of water
- Salt and pepper to taste
- 1 tbsp. butter, melted

Directions:

Add water to the pot and place a trivet. In a bowl, mix garlic, butter, salt, and pepper. Coat well. Place the bowl on the trivet. Cover the pot and cook on High for 6 minutes. Serve.

Chickpea Spread

Cook time: 18 minutes |Serves: 6| Per serving: Calories 100; Carbs 1g; Fat 4g; Protein 5g

Ingredients:

- 6 cups of water
- 1 bay leaf
- 1 cup chickpeas, soaked for 12 hours
- 2 tbsps. tahini paste
- 4 garlic cloves, minced
- Juice of 1 lemon
- ¼ tsp. cumin, ground
- A pinch of salt and black pepper

- ½ bunch parsley, chopped
- 1 tsp. sweet paprika
- A drizzle of olive oil

Directions:

Put the water and chickpeas in the pot. Add salt, black pepper, and bay leaf. Cover and cook on High for 18 minutes. Drain chickpeas, discard bay leaf and transfer to a blender. Add salt, pepper, cumin, oil, paprika, tahini paste, lemon juice, and garlic. Blend well. Transfer to a bowl and serve.

Pearl Onion Appetizer
Cook time: 6 minutes |Serves: 4| Per serving: Calories 100; Carbs 2g; Fat 2g; Protein 2g

Ingredients:

- 1-pound pearl onions, peeled
- A pinch of salt and black pepper
- ½ cup water
- 1 bay leaf
- 4 tbsps. balsamic vinegar
- 1 tbsp. coconut flour
- 1 tbsp. stevia

Directions:

In the pot, mix pearl onions with salt, pepper, water, and bay leaf. Cover and cook on Low for 5 minutes. Meanwhile, in a pan, add vinegar, stevia, and flour. Mix and bring to a simmer. Remove from heat. Pour over pearl onions. Mix and serve.

Chapter 3 Soups

Tarragon Corn Soup

Cook time: 17 minutes |Serves: 4| Per serving: Calories 361; Carbs 55.8g; Fat 11.5g; Protein 8.5g

Ingredients:

- 1 tbsp. of minced chives
- 2 tbsps. butter
- 2 finely sliced garlic cloves
- 6 corn with cobs, cut in halves
- 4 sprigs of tarragon
- 2 bay leaves
- Salt and black pepper
- Water as needed

Directions:

Melt the butter on Sauté. Add garlic and cook for 4 minutes. Add bay leaves, corn with cobs, and tarragon sprigs. Then add water to cover. Cover and cook on High for 10 minutes. Open and discard bay leaf and tarragon sprigs. Season with salt and pepper and simmer for 3 minutes. Add chives and serve.

Creamy Broccoli Soup

Cook time: 17 minutes |Serves: 2 | Per serving: Calories 140; Carbs 8.9g; Fat 10g; Protein 3.4g

Ingredients:

- 1 cup of broccoli florets, blanched
- 2 minced garlic cloves
- 2 tbsps. butter
- 1 tsp. black pepper
- 1 tbsp. of minced celery leaves
- 1 minced onion
- 1 tsp. salt
- ½ cup of full-fat milk
- ½ cup of cream
- 1 cup vegetable stock

Directions:

Melt the butter on Sauté. Add celery, garlic, and onions and cook for 4 minutes. Add broccoli, stock, salt, and pepper. Cover and cook on High for 10 minutes. Open and add milk and cream. Blend until smooth, then simmer for 3 minutes. Serve.

Creamy Mushroom Soup
Cook time: 15 minutes |Serves: 4| Per serving: Calories 210; Carbs 18g; Fat 13.6g; Protein 5g

Ingredients:

- 10 oz. finely sliced cremini mushrooms
- 3 minced garlic cloves
- 2 diced carrots
- ½ tsp. dried thyme
- ½ cup of half-and-half
- 2 tbsps. minced parsley leaves
- 2 tbsps. butter
- 1 tbsp. olive oil
- 2 stalks celery, diced
- ¼ cup of all-purpose flour
- 1 sprig of rosemary
- 1 diced onion
- 1 bay leaf

Directions:

Heat oil and butter on sauté. Add the mushrooms, carrot, celery, garlic, thyme, and onions for 4 minutes and add in the flour until light brown. Add bay leaf and close the lid. Cook on High for 10 minutes. Do a quick release and open. Stir in half and half. Season with salt, and pepper and garnish with rosemary and parsley. Serve.

Pumpkin Cream Soup
Cook time: 20 minutes |Serves: 5| Per serving: Calories 329; Carbs 24.8g; Fat 23.4g; Protein 4.8g

Ingredients:

- 2 cups of coconut cream
- 2 cups of water
- 3 cups of minced pumpkin
- ¼ tsp. ground cardamom
- 1 tsp salt
- 1 tsp. paprika
- ½ tsp. turmeric
- 1 tsp. wheat flour

- 1 peeled potato - grated

Directions:

Mix together water and flour until smooth and pour the mixture in the pot. Add the cream, chopped pumpkin, salt, paprika, cardamom, turmeric, and grated potato. Cover and cook on High for 20 minutes. Do a quick release and open. Blend with a hand mixer until smooth. Serve.

Potato Soup
Cook time: 15 minutes |Serves: 6| Per serving: Calories 117; Carbs 15g; Fat 5g; Protein 3g

Ingredients:

- 2 tbsps. olive oil
- 3 leeks, washed and drained, trimmed and thinly sliced
- 6 diced potatoes
- 4 cups of hot vegetable broth
- ½ tsp. ground nutmeg
- ½ cup milk
- Salt and pepper to taste

Directions:

Heat oil on sauté. Add leeks and sauté for 5 minutes. Add potatoes, broth, nutmeg, salt, and pepper. Cover and cook on High for 10 minutes. Open and add the milk. Blend with a hand mixer. Serve.

Turmeric Soup
Cook time: 12 minutes |Serves: 2| Per serving: Calories 341; Carbs 46g; Fat 14.8g; Protein 6.1g

Ingredients:

- ½ tsp. ground black pepper
- 1 tsp. minced garlic
- 1 tsp. grated ginger
- 1 tsp. turmeric
- 2 minced potatoes
- ½ carrot, grated
- 1 onion, grated
- 1 tsp. salt
- 1 tsp. chili flakes
- 1 oz minced celery stalk
- ½ cup of milk
- 1 cup of water

Directions:

Preheat the milk on Sauté for 3 minutes. Add the ginger, turmeric, garlic, salt, chili flakes, and black pepper. Sauté the liquid for 3 to 5 minutes or until you get a light spice smell. Add potato, carrot, onion, and celery. Add water and cover. Cook on High for 5 minutes. Open and blend with a hand mixer. Serve.

Tomato Basil Soup
Cook time: 6 minutes |Serves: 4| Per serving: Calories 200; Carbs 16g; Fat 14.1g; Protein 2.7g

Ingredients:

- 2 cups of minced tomatoes
- ¾ cup of milk
- ½ cup of vegetable broth
- ¼ tsp. baking soda
- ¼ cup of cream
- 2 tbsps. of minced basil leaves
- Salt and ground black pepper, to taste

Directions:

Add the broth and tomatoes to the pot and cover. Cook on High for 3 minutes. Do a quick release and open. Stir in baking soda and mix. Stir in milk and cream. Puree with a hand mixer. Sauté for 3 minutes and serve topped with basil.

Curried Carrot and Ginger Soup
Cook time: 17 minutes |Serves: 4| Per serving: Calories 87; Carbs 13g; Fat 3g; Protein 2g

Ingredients:

- 2 tsps. olive oil
- 2 tsps. chopped fresh ginger
- 5 large carrots, cut into bite-size pieces
- 1 tsp. curry powder
- 2 tbsps. red lentils
- 2 tsps. kosher salt
- 2 ½ cups of water

Directions:

Heat oil on Sauté. Add carrots and ginger and sauté for 2 minutes. Stir in curry powder, lentils, salt, and water. Cover and cook on High for 15 minutes. Open and blend with a hand mixer. Serve.

Chestnut Soup
Cook time: 19 minutes |Serves: 4 | Per serving: Calories 277; Carbs 36.5g; Fat 13.3g; Protein 3g

Ingredients:

- ½ pound fresh chestnuts
- 4 tbsps. butter
- 1 spring sage
- ¼ tsp. white pepper
- ¼ tsp. nutmeg
- 1 minced onion
- 1 minced stalk celery
- 1 minced potato
- 2 tbsps. rum
- 2 tbsps. fresh cream

Directions:

Puree chestnuts in a blender. Melt the butter on Sauté. Add sage, onions, celery, and white pepper in the pot and sauté for 4 minutes. Add potato, stock, and chestnuts. Cover and cook on High for 15 minutes. Open and add rum, nutmeg, and fresh cream. Blend with a hand mixer and serve.

Lentil Soup

Cook time: 12 minutes |Serves: 8| Per serving: Calories 227; Carbs 52g; Fat 3g; Protein 23g

Ingredients:

- 2 cups of dry lentils
- 6 cups of vegetable broth
- 1 medium yellow onion, diced
- 3 peeled and minced carrots
- 3 minced celery stalks
- 3 minced cloves garlic
- 1 potato, diced
- 2 tsps. herbs of Provence
- 1 tsp. olive oil
- 14 oz can of diced tomatoes in juice
- Salt and pepper to taste

Directions:

Heat oil on Sauté. Sauté the onion for 4 minutes. Then add the carrots, garlic, celery, potato, herbs, and cook for 2 minutes. Then add tomatoes, lentils, and broth. Cover and cook on High for 6 minutes. Open and season with salt and pepper. Serve.

Cauliflower Soup

Cook time: 13 minutes |Serves: 4 | Per serving: Calories 116; Carbs 9.7g; Fat 7.3g; Protein 3g

Ingredients:

- 1-pound cauliflower head
- 2 tbsps. lemon juice
- 1 tbsp. olive oil
- 1 onion, diced
- 1 tsp. salt
- ½ tsp. pepper
- ½ cup of water, for cooking
- ¼ cup cream
- 2 cups of water

Directions:

Pour 2 cups water in the pot and place the steamer rack. Place the cauliflower on the rack and cover. Cook for 5 minutes. Open and remove the cauliflower from the pot. Clean the pot and add oil and onion. Cook for 4 minutes. Then season with salt and pepper. Chop cauliflower and add into the pot. Add water and cream. Cover and cook on High for 4 minutes. Open the pot and blend with a hand mixer until smooth. Sprinkle with lemon juice and serve.

Sweet Potato and Kale Soup

Cook time: 8 minutes |Serves: 6| Per serving: Calories 384; Carbs 35.5g; Fat 26.2g; Protein 7g

Ingredients:

- 2 tbsps. olive oil
- 3 large sweet potatoes, peeled and cubed
- ½ onion, minced
- 2 garlic cloves, minced
- 1 (14-ounce) can fire-roasted tomatoes with liquid
- 1 jalapeno pepper, minced
- 1 tsp. ground turmeric
- Salt and pepper, to taste
- 14-ounce milk
- 2 cups of fresh kale, trimmed and minced
- ¼ cup of peanut butter
- 2 cups of water

Directions:

Place everything in the pot, except the kale and peanut butter. Cover and cook on High for 3 minutes. Open and stir in kale and peanut butter. Cover and cook for 5 minutes. Serve.

Butternut Squash Soup

Cook time: 20 minutes |Serves: 8| Per serving: Calories 220; Carbs 20g; Fat 14g; Protein 5.2g

Ingredients:

- 1 tbsp. extra-virgin olive oil
- ½ cup of minced onion
- 2 minced garlic cloves
- 2 pounds (1-inch chunks) butternut squash, peeled
- 3 tsps. dried oregano
- 3 tsps. kosher salt
- 1 (32-ounce) container vegetable broth
- 1 (14-ounce) can full-fat coconut milk

Directions:

Heat the oil on Sauté. Add onion and garlic and cook for 5 minutes. Add broth, squash, oregano, and salt. Cover and cook on High for 15 minutes. Do a quick release and open. Puree the soup with a hand mixer. Add the milk and cook for 5 minutes. Serve.

Tortilla and White Bean Soup
Cook time: 17 minutes |Serves: 4 | Per serving: Calories 365; Carbs 44g; Fat 14.7g; Protein 14g

Ingredients:

- 4 tbsps. butter
- 1 onion, roughly sliced
- 1 tbsp. sun-dried tomatoes
- ¼ cup of fresh cream
- 1 cup of white beans
- 4 cups of water
- ¼ tsp. white pepper
- 2 tsps. salt
- 1 minced carrot
- 4 garlic cloves, minced
- 4 tbsps. tomato paste
- Crunchy tortilla chips, for garnish

Directions:

Place the butter, carrots, onions, garlic, and white pepper in the pot and cook on Sauté for 5 minutes. Add the white beans, tomatoes, tomato paste, potatoes, salt, and water. Cover and cook on High for 12 minutes. Open and add the cream. Serve topped with tortilla chips.

Minestrone
Cook time: 12 minutes |Serves: 7 | Per serving: Calories 300; Carbs 46g; Fat 8g; Protein 11g

Ingredients:

- 3 tbsps. olive oil

- 1 onion, chopped
- 4 carrots, chopped
- 4 celery stalks, chopped
- ½ head savoy cabbage, shredded
- 1 ½ cups of cooked cannellini beans
- 1 can (14 oz) tomatoes, minced
- 1 can (14 oz) puréed tomatoes
- 2 bay leaves
- Basil, to taste
- 4 cups of vegetable broth
- Salt and pepper, to taste
- Grated Parmesan for serving

Directions:

Press Sauté and add oil. Add chopped carrots, onion, and celery. Cook for 5 minutes. Then add cabbage and cook for 3 to 4 minutes. Add the rest of the ingredients and cover. Cook on High for 4 minutes. Open and sprinkle with parmesan. Serve.

Leek Soup

Cook time: 35 minutes |Serves: 3| Per serving: Calories 224; Carbs 21g; Fat 14.4g; Protein 3g

Ingredients:

- 3 cups of leek, chopped
- 2 tbsps. coconut oil
- 1 cup of potatoes, minced
- 1 tbsp. corn flour
- ½ cup cream
- ½ cup of celery root, minced
- 3 cups of water
- 1 tsp. salt
- 1 tsp. chili flakes
- 1 tsp. minced garlic
- ½ tsp. ground ginger
- ½ tsp. white pepper
- 4 tsps. chives, minced

Directions:

Heat oil on Sauté. Add garlic, and leek and cook for 5 minutes. Add corn flour, chopped celery, cream, potatoes, chili flakes, ginger, pepper, and water. Cover and Sauté for 30 minutes. Stir and serve.

Curried Squash and Apple Soup

Cook time: 18 minutes |Serves: 6| Per serving: Calories 163; Carbs 25g; Fat 4.3g; Protein 6.4g

Ingredients:

- 2 tsps. vegetable oil
- 1 minced onion
- 3 cups of butternut squash, peeled and cubed
- 1 tsp. fresh ginger, grated finely
- 1 apple, peeled and cubed
- ¼ tsp ground turmeric
- 2 tsps. curry powder
- 1 tsp. cayenne pepper
- 4 cups of vegetable broth
- Salt and ground black pepper, to taste
- 2 ½ tbsps. of minced fresh cilantro
- 1 tbsp. fresh lemon juice

Directions:

Heat the oil on sauté. Add onion and cook for 3 minutes. Add the squash and cook for 5 minutes. Add ginger, apple, spices, and cook for 2 minutes. Add broth and cover. Cook on High for 5 minutes. Open and blend with a hand mixer. Season with salt and pepper and cook on Sauté for 3 minutes. Serve.

French Onion Soup

Cook time: 54 minutes |Serves: 8| Per serving: Calories 332; Carbs 36g; Fat 15g; Protein 14g

Ingredients:

- 3 tbsps. butter
- 2 pounds of thinly sliced onions
- 2 tsps. kosher salt
- 2 tbsps. apple cider vinegar
- 1 (32-ounce) can vegetable broth
- 1 tbsp. Worcestershire sauce
- 1 tbsp. dried thyme
- 2 dried bay leaves
- 8 slices rustic bread
- 2 cups of shredded Cheddar cheese
- ¼ cup of sugar

Directions:

Melt the butter on Sauté. Add the onions, sugar, and salt. Cook for 20 minutes. Stirring every 3-4 minutes. Place the vinegar in and deglaze the pot. Stir in broth, thyme, bay leaves, and sauce. Meantime preheat the oven to 375F. Cover the pot and cook on High for 10 minutes. Open the lid and mix. Ladle the soup into bowls and top each with cheese and a bread slice. Bake in the oven for 20 minutes. Remove the bay leaves and serve.

Chinese Noodle Soup

Cook time: 20 minutes |Serves: 7| Per serving: Calories 148; Carbs 22.6g; Fat 4.6g; Protein 4.2g

Ingredients:

- 12 oz. of cooked and drained noodles
- 20 oz. baby carrots, chopped
- 8 cups of vegetable stock
- 1 cup of red bell peppers, chopped
- 1 cup of mushrooms, chopped
- 1 cup of broccoli, chopped
- 1 cup of bok choy, chopped
- 4 green onion whites, chopped
- 8 minced garlic cloves
- 1-inch minced ginger
- 2 tsps. soy sauce
- 1 tsp. white chili vinegar
- 2 tsps. chili sauce
- 2 tbsps. olive oil
- Salt and pepper, to taste
- Green onions to taste

Directions:

Heat the oil on Sauté. Add carrots, garlic, ginger, and onions and cook for 4 minutes. Add broccoli, peppers, bok choy, mushrooms, soy sauce, chili vinegar, chili sauce, and stock. Cover and cook on High for 15 minutes. Open and add the cooked noodles. Season with black pepper and salt. Garnish with green onions and serve.

Turmeric Veggie Soup

Cook time: 20 minutes |Serves: 8 | Per serving: Calories 202; Carbs 33g; Fat 6g; Protein 4g

Ingredients:

- 4 cups of cubed butternut squash
- 2 medium sweet potatoes, peeled and cut into pieces
- 2 cups of carrots, peeled and cut into chunks
- 1 medium onion

- 2 tsps. minced garlic
- 1 tsp. grated fresh ginger
- 2 tsps. turmeric powder
- 1 tsp. garam masala
- 1 tsp. mild curry powder
- ¼ tsp. cayenne pepper
- 1 tsp. sea salt
- 3 ½ cups of vegetable broth
- 14 oz milk

Directions:

Place everything in the pot and cover. Cook on High for 20 minutes. Open and puree with a hand mixer. Serve.

Carrot Soup
Cook time: 11 minutes |Serves: 4| Per serving: Calories 154; Carbs 14g; Fat 8.4g; Protein 5.5g

Ingredients:

- ½ lemon
- 3 cups of vegetable broth
- 2 cups of minced carrot
- 1 oz of peeled, and chopped ginger
- ½ minced onion
- ¼ cup cream
- 1 tbsp. coconut oil
- 1 tsp. thyme
- 1 tsp. salt
- Pepper to taste

Directions:

Heat oil on Sauté. Add ginger and onion and cook for 5 minutes. Add carrot, thyme, salt, and mix well. Add broth and cover. Cook on High for 6 minutes. Open and smooth the mixture with a hand mixer. Add cream and sprinkle with salt. Serve.

Corn and Veggie Soup
Cook time: 12 minutes |Serves: 7| Per serving: Calories 171; Carbs 23g; Fat 5.8g; Protein 6.5g

Ingredients:

- 2 tbsps. vegetable oil
- 3 tbsps. cornstarch
- 3 peeled and minced carrots

- 2 minced celery stalks
- 1 medium onion
- 2 minced garlic cloves
- 2 peeled and minced russet potatoes
- 2 tbsps. dried parsley, crushed
- Salt and pepper, to taste
- 2 cups of fresh corn kernels
- 6 cups of vegetable broth
- ¼ cup of half-and-half

Directions:

Heat oil on Sauté. Add carrot, celery, onion, and garlic and cook for 4 minutes. Add potatoes, parsley, corn kernels, salt, black pepper, and broth. Cover and cook on High for 5 minutes. Meanwhile, mix cornstarch and half-and-half in a bowl. Remove the lid and add the cornstarch mix into the pot. Cook for 3 minutes on Sauté. Serve.

Quinoa and Vegetable Stew

Cook time: 13 minutes |Serves: 4| Per serving: Calories 217; Carbs 27.1g; Fat 5g; Protein 15.9g

Ingredients:

- 1 minced yellow onion
- 3 minced Roma tomatoes
- 1 zucchini, cut into 1-inch chunks
- ½ cup of chopped red bell pepper
- 1 ½ cups of broccoli florets
- ¼ cup of frozen corn kernels, thawed to room temperature
- ¼ cup diced carrot
- ½ cup quinoa, rinsed
- 4 tbsps. minced fresh cilantro, divided
- 1 tsp. ground coriander
- ½ tsp. ground cumin
- 2 tsps. kosher salt
- 2 tsps. corn oil
- ½ tsp. paprika
- 1 (32-ounce) container vegetable broth

Directions:

Heat oil on Sauté. Add onion and cook for 5 minutes. Add the tomatoes, corn, zucchini, bell pepper, broccoli, and carrot. Mix well. Add the quinoa, coriander, paprika, cumin, broth, salt, and 2 tbsps. cilantro. Mix well. Cover and cook on High for 8 minutes. Open and stir in 2 tbsps. cilantro. Serve.

Split Pea Soup

Cook time: 15 minutes |Serves: 6| Per serving: Calories 231; Carbs 37g; Fat 2g; Protein 17g

Ingredients:

- 5 cups of vegetable broth
- 2 cups of dried split peas
- 1 minced onion
- 1 minced green onion
- 2 minced ribs celery
- 4 cloves garlic, minced
- 3 peeled and minced potatoes
- 2 medium carrots, diced
- 2 tbsps. yeast flakes
- 1 tsp. dried basil leaves
- 1 tsp. smoked paprika
- ¼ tsp. cayenne pepper
- 1 tsp. dried thyme
- 2 bay leaves

Directions:

Place everything in the pot and cover. Cook on High for 15 minutes. Open and serve.

Cauliflower and Sweet Potato Soup

Cook time: 30 minutes |Serves: 8| Per serving: Calories 113; Carbs 20g; Fat 1.8g; Protein 5.2g

Ingredients:

- ½ tsp cumin seeds
- 3 garlic cloves, minced
- 1 tbsp. ginger paste
- 1 yellow onion, chopped
- 1 chili pepper, minced
- 4 cups veggie stock and 3 cups of water
- 1-pound sweet potatoes, cut into small cubes
- 1/8 tsp. cinnamon powder
- 1 tbsp. curry powder
- 1 cauliflower head, florets separated
- 15 ounces canned chickpeas, drained
- 15 ounces canned tomatoes, chopped
- Salt and pepper to the taste
- A pinch of cayenne pepper
- 1 tbsp. peanut butter

- 1 tbsp. oil

Directions:

Heat oil on Sauté. Add onion and brown for 3 minutes. Add ginger, cumin seeds, chili, and garlic and cook for 1 minute. Add potatoes, stock, curry powder, and cinnamon. Stir and cover. Cook on High for 20 minutes. Open and add tomatoes, chickpeas, and cauliflower. Add 3 cups of water, salt, pepper, and cayenne. Cover and cook on High for 10 minutes. Open and add peanut butter. Serve.

Black Bean Soup
Cook time: 40 minutes |Serves: 8| Per serving: Calories 240; Carbs 40 g; Fat 2.5g; Protein 12g

Ingredients:

- 1-pound black beans, soaked and drained
- 1 yellow onion, chopped
- 1 green bell pepper, chopped
- 1 red bell pepper, chopped
- 14 ounces canned tomatoes, chopped
- 3 celery stalks, chopped
- Salt and black pepper to the taste
- 1 tbsp. sweet paprika
- 1 tsp. hot sauce
- 2 tbsps. cumin
- 6 cups veggie stock
- 2 bay leaves
- 2 tbsps. chili powder
- 1 avocado, chopped for serving
- Tortilla chips for serving
- Chopped cilantro, for serving

Directions:

In the pot, mix black beans, stock, onion, bell peppers, celery, tomatoes, salt, pepper, paprika, hot sauce, cumin, chili powder, and bay leaves. Cover and cook on High for 40 minutes. Open and discard bay leaves. Divide soup among bowls. Sprinkle with cilantro, top with avocado pieces, and serve with tortilla chips.

Pearl Barley Soup
Cook time: 18 minutes |Serves: 6| Per serving: Calories 310; Carbs 43.8g; Fat 10.1g; Protein 6.6g

Ingredients:

- 1 cup all-purpose flour

- 2 onions, chopped
- 2 celery stalks, chopped
- 2 carrots, chopped
- 4 tbsps. olive oil
- 2 cups mushroom, sliced
- 28 oz. vegetable stock
- ¾ cup pearl barley
- 2 tsps. dried oregano
- 1 cup wine
- Salt and pepper, to taste

Directions:

Put the oil, garlic, and onions in the pot and press Sauté. Sauté for 3 minutes and add the rest of the ingredients. Cover and cook on High for 15 minutes. Open and serve.

Lemon Rice Soup
Cook time: 22 minutes |Serves: 6| Per serving: Calories 225; Carbs 25.5g; Fat 12g; Protein 5.1g

Ingredients:

- ¾ cup lengthy grain rice
- 1 cup onions, sliced
- 1 cup carrots, chopped
- 6 cups vegetable broth
- Salt and pepper, to taste
- ¾ cup lemon juice, freshly squeezed
- 3 tsps. minced garlic
- 1 cup celery, chopped
- 2 tbsps. olive oil
- 2 tbsps. all-purpose flour

Directions:

Put the oil, garlic, celery, and onions in the pot and press Sauté. Sauté for 4 minutes and add the rest of the ingredients except flour and lemon juice. Cover and cook on High for 12 minutes. Mix the flour and lemon juice. Open and add the lemon-flour mixture. Simmer for 5 minutes and season with salt and pepper. Serve.

Beetroot Soup
Cook time: 20 minutes |Serves: 4| Per serving: Calories 251; Carbs 27.6g; Fat 12.8g; Protein 9.2g

Ingredients:

- 2 pounds beetroot, peeled and diced

- 3 tsps. garlic, minced
- ½ cup onions, sliced
- ½ cup celery, chopped
- ½ cup carrots, chopped
- 3 tbsps. olive oil
- 4 cups vegetable broth
- 3 tbsps. fresh coriander, chopped
- Salt and pepper, to taste
- 3 tbsps. fresh cream

Directions:

Heat oil on Sauté. Add celery and onion and cook for 4 minutes. Add the rest of the ingredients except fresh cream. Cover and cook on High for 16 minutes. Open and add cream. Season with salt and pepper and garnish with coriander leaves.

Lentil and Smoked Paprika Soup

Cook time: 12 minutes |Serves: 10| Per serving: Calories 209; Carbs 39.6g; Fat 1g; Protein 11.9g

Ingredients:

- 2 cups red lentils, rinsed
- 2 cups green lentils, rinsed
- 1½ pounds of potatoes
- 1½ bunches rainbow chard
- 2 onions, chopped finely
- 4 tsps. cumin
- 2 tsps. salt
- 2 celery stalks
- 6 garlic cloves, minced
- 3 tsps. smoked paprika
- 4 carrots, sliced
- 10 cups water
- Salt and pepper, to taste

Directions:

Heat the oil on Sauté. Add garlic, celery, and onion and cook for 4 minutes. Add the rest of the ingredients. Cover and cook on High for 9 minutes. Open and season with salt and pepper. Serve.

Chapter 4 Salads

Veggie Salad

Cook time: 10 minutes |Serves: 4| Per serving: Calories 180; Carbs 20g; Fat 4g; Protein 2g

Ingredients:

- 2 yellow bell peppers, cut into thin strips
- 2 red bell peppers, cut into thin strips
- 1 red onion, chopped
- 2 tomatoes, chopped
- 1 green bell pepper, cut into thin strips
- 1 bunch parsley, chopped
- 2 garlic cloves, minced
- 1 tbsp. butter
- A pinch of salt and pepper

Directions:

Melt the butter on Sauté. Add onions and cook for 1 minute. Add bell peppers and garlic. Cook for 4 minutes. Add tomatoes, salt, pepper, and parsley. Cover and cook on High for 5 minutes. Serve.

Potato Salad

Cook time: 3 minutes |Serves: 6| Per serving: Calories 160; Carbs 24g; Fat 5g; Protein 4g

Ingredients:

- 1 small yellow onion, chopped
- 6 red potatoes
- 1 celery stalk, chopped
- 1 cup of water
- Salt and black pepper to the taste
- 3 tsps. dill, finely chopped
- 1 tsp. mustard
- 1 tsp. cider vinegar
- 3 ounces mayonnaise

Directions:

Put water and potatoes in the pot. Cover and cook on High for 3 minutes. Open and cool the potatoes. Peel and chop. Put them in a bowl. Add chopped onion celery, salt, pepper, and dill. Mix well. In a bowl, mix mayo with vinegar and mustard and mix. Add this to the salad. Mix and serve.

Red Cabbage Salad

Cook time: 5 minutes |Serves: 4| Per serving: Calories 150; Carbs 12g; Fat 2g; Protein 3g

Ingredients:

- 2 cups red cabbage, shredded
- 1 tbsp. olive oil
- Salt and black pepper to the taste
- ¼ cup white onion, finely chopped
- 2 tsps. red wine vinegar
- ½ teaspoon sugar
- Water as needed

Directions:

Put cabbage in the pot and add water. Cover and cook on High for 5 minutes. Open and drain water. Transfer cabbage to a bowl. Add salt, pepper, onion, oil, sugar, and vinegar. Mix and serve.

Brussels Sprouts Salad

Cook time: 5 minutes |Serves: 4| Per serving: Calories 170; Carbs 20.4g; Fat 8.8g; Protein 6.7g

Ingredients:

- 1-pound Brussels sprouts, trimmed and halved
- ¼ cup cashew nuts, chopped
- ½ tbsp. unsalted butter, melted
- ¼ cup almonds, chopped
- 1 cup pomegranate seeds
- 1 cup of water
- Salt and black pepper, to taste

Directions:

Place the trivet in the pot and add water. Season Brussels sprout with salt and pepper and place on the trivet. Cook on High for 4 minutes. Open and top with melted butter, almonds, cashew nuts, and pomegranate seeds. Mix and serve.

Chickpea Greek Salad

Cook time: 15 minutes |Serves: 8| Per serving: Calories 107; Carbs 8g; Fat 7g; Protein 3g

Ingredients:

- 1 cup of dried chickpeas, soaked overnight, then drained
- 3 cups of water
- 2 tbsps. extra-virgin olive oil
- 1 tbsp. red wine vinegar
- 1 tsp. kosher salt
- ½ tsp. ground black pepper
- ½ cup of finely minced onion

- 10 cherry tomatoes, cut in half
- 10 pitted black olives, cut in half
- 1 cucumber, cut into ½ -inch dice
- ¼ cup of chopped green bell pepper
- 2 tbsp. finely minced cilantro
- 1 ounce of crumbled feta cheese

Directions:

Pour the water into the pot and add the chickpeas. Cover and cook on High for 15 minutes. Open and drain. Cool. In a bowl, combine the oil, vinegar, salt, and black pepper. Mix well. In another bowl, combine the chickpeas, onion, tomatoes, olives, cucumber, bell pepper, and cilantro. Mix and top with feta. Serve.

Beans and Greens Salad
Cook time: 20 minutes |Serves: 6| Per serving: Calories 267; Carbs 29g; Fat 11g; Protein 13g

Ingredients:

- ¾ cup toasted pistachios
- 6 cups of arugula
- 3 tbsps. olive oil
- 2 tbsps. lemon juice
- 1 (15.5-ounce) can cannellini beans
- Salt and black pepper, to taste

Directions:

Place the beans, salt, and pepper in the pot and cover. Cook on High for 20 minutes. Open. In a bowl, mix the lemon juice, oil, salt, and pepper. Add beans, pistachios, and arugula. Serve.

Beet Salad
Cook time: 15 minutes |Serves: 4 | Per serving: Calories 375; Carbs 33g; Fat 16g; Protein 5.5g

Ingredients:

- 6 beets, trimmed and peeled
- 1 cup of water
- 1/4 cup balsamic vinegar
- 1/2 cup olive oil
- 1/4 tsp. salt
- 1/4 tsp. black pepper
- 1/4 cup goat's cheese
- 1/4 cup toasted walnuts
- 3 cups baby spinach

Directions:

Pour water into the pot and place in a trivet. Add the beets on top. Close and cook on High for 15 minutes. Open and chop the beets. Place in a bowl with cheese and nuts. Whisk the vinegar, oil, salt, and pepper. Pour over beets, cheese, and nuts. Mix and serve over baby spinach.

Chapter 5 Main Dishes

Lemon Grass Quinoa

Cook time: 7 minutes |Serves: 4| Per serving: Calories 200; Carbs 24g; Fat 15g; Protein 12g

Ingredients:

- ½ onion, chopped
- 1 cup quinoa, (rinsed and drained)
- 6 lemongrass stalks, each cut into 3 pieces and crushed
- ½ tsp ground coriander
- 2 cups vegetable broth
- 2 tbsps. lime juice
- 1 tbsp lemon juice
- zest from one lemon
- 1 tsp salt
- 2 tbsps. cilantro leaves, minced
- 1 tbsp. butter

Directions:

Melt the butter on Sauté. Add the onion and quinoa and cook for 5 minutes. Add the lemongrass, coriander, and broth. Mix and cover. Cook on High for 2 minutes. Open and remove the lemongrass. Add the remaining ingredients and serve.

Pumpkin, Walnut Chili

Cook time: 30 minutes |Serves: 12| Per serving: Calories 328; Carbs 42g; Fat 14g; Protein 13g

Ingredients:

- 2 cans (14.5 oz) fire-roasted tomatoes
- ½ onion, minced
- 3 cloves garlic, minced
- 2 poblano peppers, chopped
- 2 chipotle peppers, chopped
- 2 cups walnuts, chopped
- 1 cup red lentils
- 1 cup bulgur
- 2 tbsps. chili powder
- 1 tbsp smoked paprika
- 1 tbsp salt
- 6 cups of water
- 1 can (14 oz) pumpkin purée

- 2 cans (14 oz) black beans, rinsed and drained
- 1 avocado, as a garnish

Directions:

Place everything, except pumpkin puree and black beans into the pot. Cover and cook on High for 30 minutes. Open and add the remaining ingredients. Serve.

Cauliflower Quiche with Goat's Cheese

Cook time: 30 minutes |Serves: 2| Per serving: Calories 255; Carbs 6g; Fat 19.4g; Protein 15.4g

Ingredients:

- 1 cup of water
- 4 eggs
- ¼ cup of coconut milk
- ¼ cup coconut flour
- ½ cup chopped cauliflower florets
- ½ cup shredded goat's cheese divided
- 1/4 tsp. fine sea salt
- 1/4 tsp black pepper

Directions:

Place a trivet in the Instant Pot or IP and add the water. In a bowl, whisk the milk, eggs, flour, cauliflower, ¼ cup of the cheese, salt, and pepper. Pour the mixture into a soufflé dish and place it on top of the trivet. Cover and cook on High for 30 minutes. Open and sprinkle the remaining ¼ cup of the cheese on top. Serve.

Crustless Sweet Potato Quiche

Cook time: 8 minutes |Serves: 4 | Per serving: Calories 190; Carbs g; Fat 13.7g; Protein 11.6g

Ingredients:

- 4 eggs
- ¼ cup almond milk
- 1 tsp. chopped fresh parsley
- ½ tsp. salt
- 1/8 tsp. black pepper
- 2 tomatoes, seeded and diced
- ¼ cup grated sweet potato
- 4 tbsps. crumbled goat's cheese

- 2 tbsps. peeled and diced red onion
- 2 cups Water

Directions:

In a bowl, whisk milk, eggs, parsley, salt, and pepper. Stir in tomato, sweet potato, cheese, and onion. Set aside. Add egg mixture to a greased dish. Add water to the Instant Pot and place in a steam rack. Place dish on top of the steam rack. Cover and cook on High for 8 minutes. Open, slice, and serve.

Cauliflower Casserole

Cook time: 15 minutes |Serves: 4| Per serving: Calories 247; Carbs 6.1g; Fat 17.6g; Protein 19.5g

Ingredients:

- 2 cups tofu
- 2 cups chopped cauliflower
- 1 cup shredded goat's cheese
- 4 eggs, lightly beaten
- 4 tbsps. almond flour
- 4 tsps. coconut oil
- 2 tbsps. finely chopped onion
- ¼ teaspoon salt
- Additional shredded goat's cheese, optional

Directions:

Heat the oil in the Instant Pot. Add onion and cook for 5 minutes. Add all the ingredients and cover. Cook for 15 minutes on High. Open and serve.

Ratatouille

Cook time: 10 minutes |Serves: 4| Per serving: Calories 215; Carbs 32g; Fat 9.6g; Protein 6g

Ingredients:

- 2 eggplants, chopped
- 2 zucchinis, chopped
- 4 tomatoes, chopped
- 4 green bell peppers, chopped
- 4 red bell peppers, chopped
- 1 onion, chopped
- 2 garlic cloves, chopped
- 3 tbsp. oil
- ½ cup tomato sauce

- ½ tsp. thyme
- 2 tbsp. basil
- 2 tbsp. balsamic vinegar
- Salt, pepper to taste

Directions:

Heat the oil on Sauté. Cook the onion, garlic, and peppers and cook for 4 minutes. Add the zucchini, tomato, eggplant, water, thyme, salt, and peppers and brown the mixture for 4 minutes. Cover and cook for 5 minutes on High. Open and stir in basil, parsley, and seasonings. Serve.

Mac and Cheese

Cook time: 5 minutes |Serves: 6 | Per serving: Calories 430; Carbs 56g; Fat 16g; Protein 23g

Ingredients:

- 16 oz whole wheat elbow macaroni
- 4 cups vegetable broth
- 2 tbsps. butter
- 1½ tsps. garlic powder
- 2 tsps. Dijon mustard
- 1 cup cheddar cheese, shredded
- 1 cup cottage cheese
- ¼ cup Greek yogurt
- Salt and pepper to taste

Directions:

Place butter, broth, macaroni, garlic powder, and mustard into the pot. Mix and cover. Cook on High for 5 minutes. Open and stir. Add the cheddar cheese, cottage cheese, yogurt, salt, and pepper. Mix and serve.

Cauliflower Chickpea Curry

Cook time: 12 minutes |Serves: 2| Per serving: Calories 439; Carbs 68g; Fat 20g; Protein 15g

Ingredients:

- 1 tbsp butter
- ½ large red pepper, roughly chopped
- 1 can (15 oz) petite diced tomatoes, drained
- 1 cup full-fat milk
- 1 tbsp yellow curry paste
- 1 tbsp soy sauce
- ½ tbsp sugar
- 2 tsps. tapioca starch

- 1 can (15 oz) chickpeas
- 2 cups cauliflower, cut into large florets
- A squeeze of fresh lime juice
- Salt to taste
- Green onion and cilantro for garnish
- Cooked white rice for serving

Directions:

Melt the butter on Sauté. Add red pepper and cook for 2 minutes. Add tomatoes, milk, curry paste, and mix. in a bowl, mix the tapioca starch with 5 tsps. hot liquid from the pot and mix until smooth. Add this mixture to the pot. Add the soy sauce and sugar. Boil until the mixture starts to thicken. Stir in chickpeas and cauliflower. Close the pot and cook on High for 5 minutes. Open and add salt and lemon juice. Garnish and serve with rice.

Wild Rice and Basmati Pilaf
Cook time: 35 minutes |Serves: 8| Per serving: Calories 263; Carbs 36g; Fat 9g; Protein 8g

Ingredients:

- 2 tbsps. butter
- 2 brown onions, chopped
- 2 cloves garlic, minced
- 12 oz mushrooms, sliced
- ½ tsp salt
- 6 sprigs fresh thyme
- 2 cups wild rice and basmati rice mixture
- 2 cups broth
- ½ cup parsley, chopped
- ½ cup pine nuts

Directions:

Melt the butter on Sauté. Add onions and cook for 5 minutes. Add garlic and cook for 1 minute more. Add the remaining ingredients except for parsley and pine nuts. Mix and cover. Cook on High for 28 minutes. Open and stir in pine nuts and parsley. Serve.

Feta Dill Sweet Potato Mash
Cook time: 5 minutes |Serves: 4| Per serving: Calories 280; Carbs 43g; Fat 10g; Protein 8g

Ingredients:

- 4 medium sweet potatoes, peeled
- 1 cup of water
- 3 garlic cloves, peeled

- ¾ tsp kosher salt
- ¼ cup sour cream
- ¼ cup feta cheese
- 2 tsps. fresh dill
- Salt and pepper to taste

Directions:

Place sweet potatoes, garlic, salt, and water into the pot and cover. Cook on High for 5 minutes. Open and drain. Mash potatoes, stir in cream, feta, and dill. Season and serve.

Chili Garlic Noodles
Cook time: 3 minutes |Serves: 6| Per serving: Calories 286; Carbs 38g; Fat 5g; Protein 19g

Ingredients:

- 2 tbsps. butter
- ½ cup of soy sauce
- 2 tbsps. brown sugar
- 2 tbsps. white vinegar
- 1 tbsp chili garlic paste
- 2 cups of water
- 8 oz uncooked brown rice noodles
- 2 red bell peppers, thinly sliced
- Green onions, peanuts and sesame seeds for garnish

Directions:

Place everything in the pot, except red peppers and cover. Cook on High for 3 minutes. Open and mix red bell peppers. Mix, garnish, and serve.

Walnut Lentil Tacos
Cook time: 20 minutes |Serves: 4| Per serving: Calories 180; Carbs 25g; Fat 4g; Protein 7g

Ingredients:

- 1 tbsp butter
- 1 white onion, diced
- 1 clove garlic, minced
- 1 tbsp chili powder
- ½ tsp garlic powder
- ¼ tsp onion powder
- ¼ tsp red pepper flakes
- ¼ tsp oregano
- Salt and pepper to taste

- 2½ cups vegetable broth
- 1 can (15 oz) fire-roasted diced tomatoes
- ¾ cup walnuts, chopped
- 1 cup dried brown lentils
- Taco toppings: shredded lettuce, tomato, jalapeños
- 12 flour or corn tortillas

Directions:

Melt the butter on Sauté. Add onion and garlic and cook for 4 minutes. Add the spices and mix. Add the broth, lentils, tomatoes, and walnuts. Mix well. Cover and cook on High for 15 minutes. Open and season. Serve lentils on tortillas with toppings.

Penne Rigate
Cook time: 10 minutes |Serves: 5| Per serving: Calories 250; Carbs 12g; Fat 13g; Protein 3g

Ingredients:

- 15 ounces penne pasta
- 1 yellow onion, thinly sliced
- 2 garlic cloves, minced
- 12 mushrooms, thinly sliced
- 1 zucchini, thinly sliced
- A splash of sherry wine
- 1 shallot, finely chopped
- A pinch of basil, dried
- A pinch of oregano, dried
- Salt and black pepper to the taste
- 1 tbsp. butter
- 1 cup veggie stock
- 2 cups of water
- 5 ounces tomato paste
- 2 tbsps. soy sauce

Directions:

Melt the butter on Sauté. Add shallot, onion, salt, and pepper and cook for 3 minutes. Add garlic and cook for 1 minute. Add mushrooms, zucchini, basil, and oregano. Cook for 1 minute more. Add wine, stock, water, and soy sauce. Mix. Add penne, paste, more salt, and pepper. Mix and cover. Cook on High for 5 minutes. Open and serve.

Spinach Pasta
Cook time: 12 minutes |Serves: 4| Per serving: Calories 200; Carbs 18g; Fat 4g; Protein 6g

Ingredients:

- 1 pound spinach
- 1 pound fusilli pasta
- 2 garlic cloves, crushed
- 2 garlic cloves, chopped
- 1 tbsp. butter
- Salt and black pepper to the taste
- ¼ cup pine nuts, chopped
- Cheese, grated for serving
- Water as needed

Directions:

Melt the butter on Sauté. Add spinach and crushed garlic and cook for 6 minutes. Add pasta, salt, pepper, water to cover the pasta and mix. Cook on Low for 6 minutes. Open and add chopped garlic and nuts. Mix. Garnish with cheese and serve.

Pasta with Cranberry Beans

Cook time: 20 minutes |Serves: 8| Per serving: Calories 320; Carbs 61g; Fat 4g; Protein 19g

Ingredients:

- 1 tbsp. butter
- 2 cups cranberry beans, soaked in hot water for 1 hour
- 2 celery ribs, chopped
- 1 yellow onion, chopped
- Salt and black pepper to the taste
- 7 garlic cloves, minced
- 6 cups veggie stock
- 1 tsp. rosemary, chopped
- ¼ tsp. red pepper flakes
- 3 tsp. basil, dried
- 2 tsp. oregano, dried
- 26 ounces canned tomatoes, chopped
- ½ tsp. smoked paprika
- 10 ounces kale, chopped
- 2 cups small whole-grain pasta

Directions:

Melt the butter on Sauté. Add celery, onion, rosemary, red pepper flakes, and half of the garlic. Cook for 2 minutes. Add 2 tsp. basil, 1 tsp. oregano, tomatoes, and smoked paprika. Cook for 2 minutes. Add the stock, beans, salt, and pepper. Cover and cook on High for 10 minutes. Open and add the rest of the garlic, oregano, basil, pasta, kale, and more salt and pepper. Cover and cook on High for 5 minutes. Open and serve.

Shepherd's Pie

Cook time: 30 minutes |Serves: 4| Per serving: Calories 230; Carbs 43g; Fat 3g; Protein 13.2g

Ingredients:

- 26 ounces potatoes, cubed
- Water for the potatoes
- 2 tbsps. milk
- 2 tbsps. margarine
- 1 tbsp. butter
- 1 celery stick, chopped
- 1 carrot, chopped
- Salt and black pepper to the taste
- 3 ounces red lentils, already cooked
- 14 ounces canned tomatoes, chopped
- 4 ounces veggie stock

Directions:

Put the potatoes in the pot. Add water to cover the potatoes and cover the pot. Cook on High for 10 minutes. Open the drain potatoes. Transfer to a bowl. Add milk, and margarine and mash well. Clean the pot and melt the butter on Sauté. Cook celery and carrot for 2 minutes. Add lentils, stock, tomatoes, salt, and pepper and cook for 10 minutes. Add mashed potatoes and spread evenly. Cover the pot and cook on High for 6 minutes. Open and serve.

Black Bean Burgers

Cook time: 35 minutes |Serves: 5| Per serving: Calories 251; Carbs 32g; Fat 10g; Protein 10.5g

Ingredients:

- 1 cup black beans, soaked for 3 hours
- 1 tbsp. flaxseed+1 tbsp. water
- 1 red onion, chopped
- 3 tbsps. butter
- ½ cup quick oats
- ½ tsp. cumin
- 2 tsps. chipotle powder
- Salt to taste
- 2 garlic cloves, minced
- 2 tsps. lemon zest, grated
- Burger buns for serving
- Red cabbage, thinly sliced for serving
- Water for cooking

Directions:

Drain beans and place them in the pot. Cover the beans with water and cover the pot. Cook on High for 20 minutes. Open and drain the beans again. Put them in a bowl. Crush with a fork and set aside. Clean the pot and melt 1 tbsp. butter on Sauté. Add onion and cook for 3 minutes. Add garlic and cook for 3 minutes more. Remove and add to the bowl with the beans. Add flaxseed plus water, oats, cumin, chipotle powder, salt, and lemon zest. Mix well and make 5 burgers. Heat the rest of the butter in the pot and cook burgers 3 minutes per side on Sauté. Divide on burger buns and, add red cabbage and serve.

Black Eyed Peas Patties
Cook time: 30 minutes |Serves: 10 | Per serving: Calories 200; Carbs 31g; Fat 6.2g; Protein 8g

Ingredients:

- 1 and ½ cups black-eyed peas, soaked overnight and drained
- 4 cups of water
- 1 tsp. red chili paprika
- 4 tbsps. coriander, finely chopped
- Salt to the taste
- 5 garlic cloves, grated
- 1 tsp. cumin powder
- 2 tbsps. toasted sesame seeds
- 2 tbsps. butter
- 1 cup onion, chopped and pickled in some vinegar
- Burger buns
- 1 cup tomatoes, sliced

Directions:

Put peas in the pot. Add water and cover. Cook on High for 20 minutes. Drain and transfer peas to a bowl. Mash them a bit with a fork. Add paprika, coriander, salt, garlic, cumin, sesame seeds and mix well and form 10 patties. Clean the pot and melt the butter on Sauté. Cook the patties 3 to 4 minutes per side. Arrange the burgers and serve with pickled onions and tomato slices.

Chickpea Burgers
Cook time: 22 minutes |Serves: 6| Per serving: Calories 120; Carbs 20g; Fat 4g; Protein 6g

Ingredients:

- 1 cup dried chickpeas, soaked for 4 hours
- 1 tsp. thyme, dried
- 1 tsp. cumin
- 2 bay leaves
- 1 tsp. onion salt

- 1 tsp. garlic powder
- Black pepper to the taste
- 3 tbsps. tomato paste
- ½ cup whole wheat flour
- 1 tbsp. butter
- Water as needed

Directions:

Drain chickpeas and put them in the pot. Add water to cover, cumin powder, bay leaves, garlic powder, thyme, onion salt, and black pepper. Cover and cook on High for 15 minutes. Open, discard bay leaves, drain water, and transfer chickpeas to a food processor and pulse well. Add tomato paste and flour and blend again. Make 5 patties. Melt the butter on Sauté in the pot. Cook the patties, 3 minutes per side. Serve.

Mushroom Patties
Cook time: 22 minutes |Serves: 6| Per serving: Calories 170; Carbs 14g; Fat 6g; Protein 14g

Ingredients:

- 1 tbsp. oil
- 1 garlic clove, minced
- 3 green onions, minced
- 1 yellow onion, minced
- ½ tsp. cumin
- 15 ounces canned pinto beans, drained
- ¾ cup mushrooms, chopped
- 1 tsp. parsley leaves, chopped
- Salt and black pepper to the taste
- Butter for frying

Directions:

Heat the oil on Sauté. Add garlic and yellow onion and cook for 5 minutes. Add mushroom, green onions, salt, pepper, and cumin. Cover and cook on Low for 5 minutes. Open and transfer mushrooms mix to a bowl. Set aside. Put the beans in a food processor and blend a few times. Add them to the mushroom mix. Add more salt and pepper to the taste and parsley and mix well. Shape patties. Melt butter on Sauté and cook the patties 3 minutes per side. Serve.

Smokey Amaranth Burgers
Cook time: 16 minutes |Serves: 6| Per serving: Calories 260; Carbs 23g; Fat 8g; Protein 12g

Ingredients:

- ¼ cup amaranth

- ¾ cup of water
- A pinch of smoked paprika
- A pinch of thyme, dried
- 15 ounces canned black beans, drained
- 1 green chili pepper, chopped
- ½ red bell pepper, chopped
- Salt to the taste
- ½ tsp. garlic powder
- ½ tsp. chipotle pepper powder
- ½ tsp. parsley, dried
- ½ tsp. onion flakes
- 2 tbsp. breadcrumbs
- 1 tbsp. butter

Directions:

Toast the amaranth for 1 minute on Sauté. Add water, salt, paprika, and thyme. Mix and cover. Cook on High for 10 minutes. Open and drain. Mash beans a bit and add them to the amaranth. Add chili pepper, red bell pepper, salt, garlic powder, chipotle powder, parsley, onion flakes, and breadcrumbs and mix well. Make patties. Heat the butter in the pot and cook the patties 3 minutes per side. Serve.

Broccoli Burgers

Cook time: 23 minutes |Serves: 6| Per serving: Calories 190; Carbs 16g; Fat 8g; Protein 10g

Ingredients:

- ½ cup pink lentils, soaked and drained
- 1 cup broccoli florets
- ½ cup tomato, chopped
- 1/3 tsp. garlic powder
- ¾ cup of water
- Salt to the taste
- 1 and ½ cups pinto beans, already cooked
- 1 tsp. chipotle powder
- ¼ tsp. cumin powder
- ½ tsp. paprika
- A pinch of cayenne pepper
- 1 tbsp. parsley, chopped
- 4 drops lemon juice
- ¼ cup red onion, chopped
- 3 tbsps. chickpea flour
- 1 tbsp. butter

Directions:

Put lentils in the pot, add salt, water, and tomato. Cover and cook on High for 7 minutes. Open and add broccoli. Cover and cook on High for 10 minutes more. Open and discard water if needed. Put everything in a bowl and mash with a fork. Mash the pinto beans with a fork and add them in the bowl. Add garlic powder, chipotle, powder, cumin powder, paprika, cayenne, parsley, onion, lemon juice, flour, and more salt to taste. Mix and make patties. Clean the pot and melt the butter on Sauté. Cook the patties in the pot for 3 minutes per side. Serve.

Couscous Patties
Cook time: 16 minutes |Serves: 6| Per serving: Calories 160; Carbs 33g; Fat 4g; Protein 9g

Ingredients:

- ½ tsp. sesame oil
- 1 cup couscous, rinsed
- ¼ cup red bell pepper, finely chopped
- ½ cup red onion, finely chopped
- Salt and black pepper to taste
- 1 and ½ cups veggie stock
- ½ tsp. cinnamon, ground
- ¼ tsp. coriander, ground
- 2 tbsp. wine vinegar
- 1 tbsp. flaxseed mixed well with 2 tbsps. water
- ½ cup brown rice flour
- Butter for frying

Directions:

Heat the sesame oil on Sauté. Add red bell pepper and onion and cook for 4 minutes. Add couscous, stock, salt, pepper, coriander, vinegar, and cinnamon. Cover and cook on High for 4 minutes. Open and fluff couscous, transfer it to a bowl. Add flaxseed mixed with water and mix everything. Make 6 burgers and dust with rice flour. Clean the pot and melt the butter. Cook the burgers 4 minutes per side. Serve.

Spinach Curry
Cook time: 15 minutes |Serves: 3| Per serving: Calories 210; Carbs 36g; Fat 5g; Protein 10g

Ingredients:

- 1 tsp. butter
- 1/3 cup brown lentils
- 1 small ginger piece, grated
- 4 garlic cloves, minced
- 1 green chili pepper, chopped

- 2 tomatoes, chopped
- ½ tsp. garam masala
- ½ tsp. turmeric powder
- 2 potatoes, cubed
- A pinch of salt and black pepper
- ¼ tsp. cardamom, ground
- ¼ tsp. cinnamon powder
- 1 cup of water
- 6 ounces of spinach leaves

Directions:

Melt the butter on Sauté. Add chili pepper, ginger, and garlic. Cook for 3 minutes. Add tomatoes, salt, pepper, cinnamon, cardamom, turmeric, and garam masala. Cook for 4 minutes. Add lentils, potatoes, water, and spinach. Cover and cook on High for 8 minutes. Open and serve.

Brown Rice Stew

Cook time: 25 minutes |Serves: 2| Per serving: Calories 210; Carbs 10g; Fat 8g; Protein 12g

Ingredients:

- 2 tsps. butter
- ½ cup brown rice
- ½ cup mung beans
- ½ tsp. cumin seeds
- ½ cup red onion, chopped
- 2 tomatoes, chopped
- 1 small ginger piece, grated
- 4 garlic cloves, minced
- 1 tsp. coriander, ground
- ½ tsp. turmeric
- A pinch of cayenne pepper
- ½ tsp. garam masala
- 4 cups of water
- A pinch of salt and black pepper
- 1 tsp. lemon juice

Directions:

In the blender, mix tomato with garlic, onions, ginger, salt, pepper, garam masala, cayenne, coriander, and turmeric and pulse well. Melt the butter on Sauté. Add tomato mixture and cook for 15 minutes. Add mung beans, rice, water, lemon juice, and cumin. Mix and cover. Cook on High for 10 minutes. Serve.

Quinoa and Veggie Mix

Cook time: 16 minutes |Serves: 3| Per serving: Calories 140; Carbs 18g; Fat 6g; Protein 10g

Ingredients:

- 1 yellow onion, chopped
- 2 tbsps. butter
- 2 small carrots, shredded
- 2 cups button mushrooms, sliced
- 2 tbsps. lemon juice
- Zest from ½ lemon, grated
- 4 garlic cloves minced
- A pinch of salt and black pepper
- 1 cup red quinoa
- 10 cherry tomatoes, halved
- 1 cup veggie stock
- 1 tbsp. parsley, chopped

Directions:

Melt the butter on Sauté. Add carrot and onion and cook for 2 minutes. Add mushrooms and cook for 4 minutes more. Add lemon juice, lemon zest, stock, salt, pepper, quinoa, and tomatoes. Mix and cover. Cook on High for 10 minutes. Add parsley and serve.

Sweet Potato Stew

Cook time: 10 minutes |Serves: 4| Per serving: Calories 300; Carbs 12g; Fat 9g; Protein 7g

Ingredients:

- 1 small yellow onion, chopped
- 1 tbsp. butter
- 2 garlic cloves, minced
- A small ginger piece, grated
- 2 sweet potatoes, chopped
- 1 zucchini, chopped
- 1 red bell pepper, chopped
- 14 ounces canned tomatoes, chopped
- 1 tsp. turmeric powder
- 2 tsps. curry powder
- A pinch of salt and black pepper
- 2 tbsps. red curry paste
- 14 ounces milk
- Juice from 3 limes
- 1 tbsp. cilantro, chopped

Directions:

Melt the butter on Sauté. Add onion and cook for 3 minutes. Add garlic and ginger and cook for 1 minute more. Add sweet potatoes, zucchini, bell pepper, tomatoes, turmeric, curry powder, curry paste, salt, pepper, milk, and cover. Cook on High for 5 minutes. Add lime juice and cilantro. Serve.

Split Pea Stew
Cook time: 14 minutes |Serves: 4 | Per serving: Calories 312; Carbs 12g; Fat 6g; Protein 7g

Ingredients:

- 1 carrot, cubed
- 1 yellow onion, chopped
- 1 and ½ tbsps. butter
- 1 celery stick, chopped
- 5 garlic cloves, minced
- 1 bay leaf
- 1 and ½ tsp.. cumin, ground
- 1 tsp. sweet paprika
- ¼ tsp. chili powder
- A pinch of salt and black pepper
- ¼ tsp. cinnamon powder
- ½ cup tomatoes, chopped
- Juice of ½ lemon
- 2 cups yellow peas
- 1-quart veggie stock
- 1 tbsp. chives, chopped

Directions:

Melt the butter on Sauté. Add carrots, onion, and celery and cook for 4 minutes. Add the garlic, bay leaf, cumin, paprika, chili powder, salt, pepper, cinnamon, tomatoes, lemon juice, peas, and stock. Cover and cook on High for 10 minutes. Open and add chives. Mix and serve.

Veggie Stew
Cook time: 15 minutes |Serves: 5 | Per serving: Calories 261; Carbs 18g; Fat 7g; Protein 8g

Ingredients:

- 2 tbsps. butter
- 2 carrots, chopped
- 1 yellow onion, chopped
- 3 potatoes, chopped
- 14 ounces green beans
- 2 garlic cloves, minced

- 14 ounces canned tomatoes, chopped
- 1 cup of corn
- 1 cup peas
- 1 bay leaf
- 5 cups of water
- A pinch of salt and black pepper
- 1 tbsp. parsley, chopped

Directions:

Melt the butter on Sauté. Add onion and cook for 5 minutes. Add carrots, potatoes, green beans, garlic, tomatoes, corn, peas, bay leaf, salt, pepper, and water. Cover and cook on High for 10 minutes. Add parsley and mix. Serve.

Mushroom Mix
Cook time: 15 minutes |Serves: 3| Per serving: Calories 321; Carbs 16g; Fat 5g; Protein 8g

Ingredients:

- 4 garlic cloves, minced
- 2 red chili peppers, chopped
- 1 tsp. butter
- 1 bay leaf
- 1 yellow onion, chopped
- 2 chipotle chilies in adobo sauce
- 1 tsp. cumin, ground
- ½ tsp. oregano, dried
- ½ tsp. smoked paprika
- A pinch of salt and black pepper
- ¼ tsp. cinnamon powder
- 1 cup veggie stock
- 8 ounces white mushrooms, sliced
- 3 tsps. lime juice
- 1 tsp. apple cider vinegar

Directions:

Melt the butter on Sauté. Add bay leaf, garlic, onion, salt, and pepper. Cook for 5 minutes. Add the rest of the ingredients and cover. Cook on High for 10 minutes. Serve.

Creamy Tofu Marsala Pasta
Cook time: 15 minutes |Serves: 2| Per serving: Calories 440; Carbs 46g; Fat 20g; Protein 19g

Ingredients:

- 1 tbsp. butter
- ½ tsp. garlic powder
- 1 small diced onion
- 2 cups of mushrooms, sliced
- ½ cup of sun-dried tomatoes
- ½ cup of tofu, diced into chunks
- 1 ½ cups of vegetable broth
- 1 cup of white Marsala wine
- 1 cup of Pennette pasta
- ½ cup of grated goat's cheese
- ¼ cup of cream

Directions:

Melt the butter on Sauté. Add onion and mushrooms and cook for 4 minutes. Add the tofu and tomatoes and cook for 3 minutes. Put in the garlic powder and cook for 1 minute. Add the white wine and cook for 1 minute. Place the broth and mix. Place the pasta, don't stir. Cover and cook on High for 6 minutes. Add the cream and cheese and let sit for 5 minutes. Serve.

Minty Pea Risotto
Cook time: 22 minutes |Serves: 2| Per serving: Calories 370; Carbs 50g; Fat 14.8g; Protein 9.3g

Ingredients:

- 2 tbsps. butter
- 1 peeled and diced onion
- ½ tsp. garlic powder
- ½ cup of fresh peas
- ½ cup of barley
- 1 cup of vegetable broth divided
- ¼ tsp. lime zest
- Ground black pepper to taste
- ¼ cup of chopped fresh mint leaves
- 1 carrot, chopped

Directions:

Melt the butter on Sauté. Cook onion for 5 minutes. Add garlic and barley and cook for 1 minute more. Add ½ cup broth and cook 3 minutes or until absorbed by barley. Add remaining broth, salt, and pepper. Cover and cook for 10 minutes on High. Add lemon zest, mint, and peas. Heat 3 minutes and serve.

Tofu Pulao
Cook time: 18 minutes |Serves: 4| Per serving: Calories 447; Carbs 68.8g; Fat 20.5g; Protein 29g

Ingredients:

-

Directions:

Melt the butter on Sauté. Add the cumin seeds and fry well. Add the onions and green chilies. Cook for 4 minutes. Add ginger-garlic paste and cook for 2 minutes. Add the tomatoes and cook for 3 minutes. Add the turmeric, coriander, red chili powder, salt, and garam masala and mix well. Add tofu, rice, water, and mix. Cook on High for 6 minutes. Open and garnish with mint. Serve.

Chapter 6 Grains, Rice, Beans, Legumes, and Lentils

Veggie and Rice Dish
Cook time: 15 minutes |Serves: 4| Per serving: Calories 270; Carbs 1.2g; Fat 2.6g; Protein 5.5g

Ingredients:

- 2 cups long-grain rice
- 1 red bell pepper, thinly sliced
- 1 tbsp. olive oil
- 1 yellow onion, finely chopped
- 1 carrot, grated
- Salt and black pepper to the taste
- 4 cups of water
- ½ cup peas

Directions:

Heat oil on Sauté. Add onions and cook for 4 minutes. Add rice, water, bell pepper, carrot, peas, salt, and pepper. Cook on High for 10 minutes. Open and serve.

Millet and Veggies
Cook time: 25 minutes |Serves: 4| Per serving: Calories 170; Carbs 12g; Fat 7g; Protein 14g

Ingredients:

- ½ cup oyster mushrooms, thinly sliced
- 1 cup millet, soaked and drained
- 1 cup leeks, finely chopped
- 2 garlic cloves, minced
- 1 tsp. vegetable oil
- ½ cup green lentils, rinsed
- ½ cup bok choy, sliced
- 2 and ¼ cups veggie stock
- 1 cup asparagus, cut into medium pieces
- 1 cup snow peas, sliced
- ¼ cup mixed chives and parsley, finely chopped
- A drizzle of lemon juice
- Salt and black pepper to the taste

Directions:

Heat oil on Sauté. Cook mushrooms, leeks, and garlic for 3 minutes. Add lentils and millet. Cook for 4 minutes. Add bok choy, asparagus, snow peas, and veggie stock. Cover and cook on High for

10 minutes. Open and season with salt and pepper. Divide among bowls. Sprinkle with lemon juice, chives, and parsley and serve.

Lentils and Rice Risotto
Cook time: 15 minutes |Serves: 6| Per serving: Calories 190; Carbs 35g; Fat 2.5g; Protein 5.7g

Ingredients:

- 1 tbsp. olive oil
- 1 cup arborio rice
- 1 cup lentils, soaked overnight
- 1 yellow onion, finely chopped
- 1 celery stalk, finely chopped
- Salt and black pepper to the taste
- 1 tbsp. parsley, finely chopped
- 3 and ¼ cup veggie stock
- 2 garlic cloves, crushed

Directions:

Heat oil on Sauté. Add onions and cook for 4 minutes. Add celery and parsley and cook for 1 minute. Add garlic, rice, stock, and lentils. Cover and cook on High for 10 minutes. Open and serve.

Farro with Mushrooms and Beans
Cook time: 30 minutes |Serves: 3| Per serving: Calories 240; Carbs 40g; Fat 6.6g; Protein 11g

Ingredients:

- 2 tbsps. barley
- ½ cup farro
- 1 cup navy beans, dried, soaked overnight, and drained
- 3 cups mushrooms, chopped
- 1 tbsp. red curry paste
- 1 jalapeno pepper, seeded and chopped
- 1 tbsp. shallot powder
- 2 tbsps. onion powder
- Salt and pepper to the taste
- 4 garlic cloves, minced
- 2 tomatoes, diced
- Water as needed
- Chopped cilantro for serving
- Chopped scallions for serving

Directions:

Put beans, farro, and barley in the pot. Add mushrooms, garlic, jalapeno, curry paste, shallot, onion powder, salt, pepper to the taste, and water to cover all the ingredients. Cover the pot and cook on High for 30 minutes. Do a quick release and open. Add tomatoes and mix. Sprinkle with cilantro and scallions and serve.

Polenta

Cook time: 10 minutes |Serves: 3| Per serving: Calories 200; Carbs 13g; Fat 4.5g; Protein 14g

Ingredients:

- 2 cups very hot water
- 1 bunch of green onions, thinly sliced
- 2 cups veggie stock
- 2 tsps. garlic, minced
- 1 tbsp. chili powder
- 1 cup cornmeal
- ¼ cup cilantro, finely chopped
- Salt and black pepper to the taste
- 1 tsp. cumin
- 1 tsp. oregano
- A pinch of cayenne pepper
- ½ tsp. smoked paprika
- 2 tsps. oil

Directions:

Heat the oil on Sauté. Add the green onion and garlic and cook for 2 minutes. Add stock, hot water, cornmeal, cilantro, salt, pepper, chili powder, cumin, oregano, paprika, and cayenne pepper. Close the pot and cook on High for 10 minutes. Open and serve.

Quinoa Pilaf

Cook time: 10 minutes |Serves: 4| Per serving: Calories 160; Carbs 15g; Fat 5.7g; Protein 7g

Ingredients:

- ½ cup yellow onion, finely chopped
- 1 and ½ cups quinoa, washed and drained
- 1 tbsp. butter
- 14 ounces canned veggie stock
- 1 celery stalk, finely chopped
- Salt to the taste
- ¼ cup of water
- 2 tbsps. parsley leaves, chopped
- ½ cup almonds, sliced and toasted

Directions:

Melt the butter on Sauté in the pot. Add onions and celery and cook for 5 minutes. Add stock, water, quinoa, and salt. Cover and cook on High for 3 minutes. Open and fluff the quinoa with a fork. Sprinkle with parsley and almonds serve.

Curried Sorghum
Cook time: 20 minutes |Serves: 4| Per serving: Calories 300; Carbs 20g; Fat 6g; Protein 23g

Ingredients:

- 3 cups of water
- 1 cup sorghum
- 1 cup milk
- Salt to the taste
- 3 tbsps. rice wine vinegar
- ½ tsp. chili powder
- 1 tbsp. curry powder
- 2 cups carrots
- ½ cup golden raisins
- ¼ cup green onion, finely chopped
- 2 tsps. sugar

Directions:

Put the sorghum, water, and salt in the pot. Cover and cook on High for 20 minutes. In a bowl, mix sugar, milk, vinegar, salt, curry powder, and chili powder and mix well. Drain sorghum and transfer to a bowl. Add milk mix, carrots, onions, and raisins. Mix and serve.

Couscous with Mint
Cook time: 8 minutes |Serves: 4 | Per serving: Calories 260; Carbs 23g; Fat 7g; Protein 10g

Ingredients:

- 1 cup pearl couscous
- 2 tbsps. extra virgin olive oil
- 1 small yellow onion, thinly sliced
- 1 and ½ cups veggie stock
- 2/3 cup green peas
- ¼ cup cheese, grated
- 2 tbsps. mint leaves, finely chopped
- Salt and black pepper to the taste

Directions:

Heat oil on Sauté. Add onion and cook for 3 minutes. Add stock, couscous, peas, salt, and pepper. Stir and cover. Cook on High for 5 minutes. Open and add cheese and mint. Mix and serve.

Kidney beans with Veggies

Cook time: 45 minutes |Serves: 4| Per serving: Calories 213; Carbs 34.5g; Fat 4.3g; Protein 11.4g

Ingredients:

- 1 cup kidney beans, soaked overnight
- 1 medium carrot, chopped
- 1 cup tomatoes, chopped
- 3 tbsps. fresh basil
- 1 tsp. thyme
- 1 tsp. red pepper flakes
- 1 small onion, sliced
- 3 garlic cloves, minced
- 1 tbsp. olive oil
- 1 tsp. oregano
- 2 cups of water
- Salt and black pepper, to taste

Directions:

Press Sauté and add oil, garlic, and onions in the pot. Cook for 4 minutes. Add red pepper flakes, oregano, basil, thyme, salt, and pepper. Sauté for 1 minute and add tomatoes, carrots, water, and beans. Cover and cook on High for 40 minutes. Open and serve.

Chickpeas with Parsley

Cook time: 27 minutes |Serves: 3| Per serving: Calories 228; Carbs 25.8g; Fat 11.7g; Protein 7.9g

Ingredients:

- 1 cup chickpeas, soaked overnight
- 2 cups of water
- 1 small onion, sliced
- 2 garlic cloves, minced
- 2 tbsps. olive oil
- ¼ cup parsley, chopped
- ¼ cup dill leaves, chopped
- 2 tbsps. fresh lemon juice
- 1 tsp. salt

Directions:

Add oil and press Sauté. Add onion and garlic and cook for 2 minutes. Add everything except for the parsley and lemon juice. Cover and cook on High for 25 minutes. Open and add lemon juice and parsley. Serve.

Kidney Bean Curry
Cook time: 28 minutes |Serves: 3| Per serving: Calories 427; Carbs 64g; Fat 17.5g; Protein 20g

Ingredients:

- 1 cup dried red kidney beans, soaked for overnight and drained
- ¼ cup split chickpeas, soaked for overnight and drained
- 4 cups of water
- 3 tbsps. olive oil
- 3 tsps. garlic, minced
- 1 large tomato, chopped finely
- 2 medium onions, chopped
- 3 tsps. fresh ginger, minced
- 1½ tsps. ground coriander
- 1½ tsps. ground turmeric
- 1½ tsps. ground cumin
- 2 tsps. red chili powder
- ¼ tsp. salt
- 4 tbsps. fresh cilantro, chopped

Directions:

Put the oil, garlic, ginger, and onions in the pot and press Sauté. Sauté for 4 minutes. Add coriander, turmeric, cumin, red chili powder, and salt. Sauté for 4 minutes. Add water, tomatoes, beans, and chickpeas. Cover and cook on High for 20 minutes. Open, garnish, and serve.

Lentil Curry
Cook time: 20 minutes |Serves: 4| Per serving: Calories 354; Carbs 54.8g; Fat 6.5g; Protein 20.6g

Ingredients:

- 1½ cups lentils, rinsed
- 1 tbsp. garlic, minced
- 1½ tbsps. lemon juice
- 1½ tbsps. ginger, minced
- 4 cups of water
- 1½ tsps. salt
- 1½ tsps. cumin seeds
- 3 medium tomatoes, chopped
- 1½ tbsp. oil

- 2 medium onions, diced
- Cilantro, to garnish

Directions:

Add the oil, cumin, garlic, and onions in the Instant Pot and cook on Sauté for 4 minutes. Add rest of the ingredients except for lime juice and cilantro. Cover and cook on High for 15 minutes. Do a quick release. Open and add lime juice and cilantro. Serve.

Chickpea, White Bean and Tomato Stew

Cook time: 30 minutes |Serves: 4| Per serving: Calories 432; Carbs 69.6g; Fat 12.6g; Protein 30.4g

Ingredients:

- 1 cup dried white beans, soaked overnight
- 1 cup dried chickpeas, soaked overnight
- ¼ cup dried red lentils
- 1 medium yellow onion, chopped
- 1½ cups tomatoes, diced
- 2 tbsps. tomato paste
- 2 tbsps. olive oil
- 2 stalks celery, thinly sliced
- 2 tsps. dried dill
- 2 tsps. ground cinnamon
- 2 tbsps. mild paprika
- 2 tsps. ground cumin
- 1 tsp. salt
- 1 tsp. ground black pepper
- 3 cups vegetable broth

Directions:

Heat the oil on Sauté in the pot. Add celery and onions and cook for 4 minutes. Add dill, cinnamon, paprika, cumin, salt, and black pepper. Sauté for 2 minutes and add chickpeas, beans, tomatoes, lentils, and tomato paste. Cover and cook on High for 20 minutes. Open and serve.

Spinach Split Pea

Cook time: 10 minutes |Serves: 3| Per serving: Calories 147; Carbs 23g; Fat 3.1g; Protein 8.3g

Ingredients:

- 1 cup spinach, chopped
- ½ cup split pea, washed
- ¼ tsp. cumin seeds
- 2 garlic cloves, finely chopped

- 1½ cups water
- ½ tbsp. oil
- ½ inch ginger, finely chopped
- 1 tomato, chopped
- ½ tsp. salt

Directions:

Add the oil, garlic, ginger, and cumin in the pot and press Sauté. Cook for 1 minute and add tomato paste and salt. Add water and peas and mix. Cover and cook on High for 5 minutes. Open and add spinach. Cook on Sauté for 3 minutes. Serve.

Confetti Rice

Cook time: 11 minutes |Serves: 4| Per serving: Calories 333; Carbs 40.6g; Fat 13.5g; Protein 13.2g

Ingredients:

- 1 cup lengthy grain white rice
- 3 cups frozen peas, thawed
- 3 tbsps. butter
- 2 cloves garlic, minced
- 1 cup vegetable broth
- ¼ cup lemon juice
- 1 small onion, chopped
- 1 tbsp. cumin powder
- ½ tsp. salt
- ½ tsp. black pepper

Directions:

Put the butter and onions in the pot and press Sauté. Sauté for 3 minutes and add the rest of the ingredients. Cover and cook on High for 8 minutes. Open and serve.

Coconut Rice

Cook time: 8 minutes |Serves: 4| Per serving: Calories 353; Carbs 26.8g; Fat 16.9g; Protein 3.7g

Ingredients:

- 1 cup unsweetened coconut, grated
- 1½ cups of lengthy grain white rice
- 3 tbsps. butter
- 3 cups water
- ½ cup currants
- 1 tsp. cinnamon powder
- ¼ tsp. cloves

- ¾ tsp. salt

Directions:

Press Sauté and add butter. Add everything except for rice and water. Cook for 2 minutes and add rice and water. Cover and cook on High for 6 minutes. Open and serve.

Bok Choy Rice

Cook time: 26 minutes |Serves: 5 | Per serving: Calories 286; Carbs 53.4g; Fat 3.4g; Protein 5.6g

Ingredients:

- 1½ cups of rice
- 3 cups chopped bok choy, leaves and stems trimmed
- 1 tbsp. olive oil
- ½ cup garlic, chopped
- ½ cup onions, chopped
- 3 cups hot vegetable broth
- ½ cup white wine
- ½ tsp. red pepper flakes
- ½ tsp. salt

Directions:

Add oil and cook onions and garlic on Sauté for 4 minutes. Add the rest of the ingredients and cover. Cook on High for 22 minutes. Open and serve.

Creamy Mushroom Alfredo Rice

Cook time: 25 minutes |Serves: 4| Per serving: Calories 332; Carbs 42.1g; Fat 15.4g; Protein 7g

Ingredients:

- 1 cup of rice
- 2 tbsps. olive oil
- 2 ¾ cups of vegetable stock
- ¾ cup onions, finely chopped
- 2 garlic cloves, minced
- 1½ tbsps. fresh lemon juice
- 2 oz. creamy mushroom Alfredo sauce
- Salt and black pepper, to taste
- ¼ cup walnuts, coarsely chopped

Directions:

Put the oil, onions, and garlic in the pot and press Sauté. Sauté for 3 minutes and add rice and broth. Cover and cook on High for 22 minutes. Open and add lemon juice, salt, pepper, and sauce. Garnish and serve.

Spinach Mushroom Pesto Pasta
Cook time: 10 minutes |Serves: 4| Per serving: Calories 457; Carbs 62g; Fat 17g; Protein 14g

Ingredients:

- 1 tbsp. oil
- 8 oz minced mushrooms
- ½ tsp. black ground pepper
- ½ tsp. kosher salt
- 8 oz uncooked spaghetti pasta
- 5 oz. spinach
- 1 ¾ cups water
- ½ cup of pesto
- 1/3 cup of parmesan grated cheese

Directions:

Press Sauté and add oil, mushrooms, salt, and pepper. Cook for 5 minutes. Add pasta and water. Cover and cook on High for 5 minutes. Open and stir in spinach, pesto, and cheese. Mix and serve.

Wild Rice and Basmati Pilaf
Cook time: 35 minutes |Serves: 6 | Per serving: Calories 263; Carbs 35.4g; Fat 9.5g; Protein 9g

Ingredients:

- 2 minced brown onions
- 2 minced cloves garlic
- 12 oz mushrooms, sliced
- ½ tsp. salt
- 2 tbsps. olive oil
- 6 sprigs fresh thyme
- 2 cups of broth
- 2 cups of wild rice and basmati rice mixture
- Chopped pine nuts and minced parsley for garnish

Directions:

Heat oil on Sauté. Add onions and cook for 6 minutes. Then add minced garlic and cook for 1 minute. Add the remaining ingredients and cover. Cook on High for 28 minutes. Open and add parsley and pine nuts. Serve.

Endives and Rice Soup

Cook time: 27 minutes |Serves: 4| Per serving: Calories 200; Carbs 20g; Fat 7g; Protein 6g

Ingredients:

- 1 tbsp. butter
- 2 tsps. sesame oil
- 2 scallions, chopped
- 3 garlic cloves chopped
- 1 tbsp. ginger, grated
- 1 tsp. chili sauce
- A pinch of salt and black pepper
- ½ cup white rice
- 6 cups veggie stock
- 3 endives, trimmed and chopped

Directions:

Melt the butter on Sauté and add the sesame oil. Add garlic, scallions, ginger, and chili sauce. Cook for 5 minutes. Add stock and rice, mix and cover. Cook on High for 17 minutes. Add salt, pepper, and endives, stir, and cover. Cook on High for 5 minutes more. Serve.

Barley and Spinach Pesto

Cook time: 20 minutes |Serves: 4| Per serving: Calories 200; Carbs 8g; Fat 5g; Protein 4g

Ingredients:

- 1 cup barley
- 2 and ½ cups of water
- 1 cup spinach pesto
- 1 green apple, chopped
- ¼ cup celery, chopped
- Salt and black pepper to the taste

Directions:

Put barley, water, salt, and pepper in the pot. Mix and cover. Cook on High for 20 minutes. Drain and transfer to a bowl. Add celery, apple, spinach pesto, and add more salt and pepper if necessary. Mix and serve.

Rice and Chickpeas Bowl

Cook time: 28 minutes |Serves: 4| Per serving: Calories 292; Carbs 9g; Fat 6g; Protein 10g

Ingredients:

- 1 tbsp. butter

- 2 tbsps. chana masala
- 1 red onion, chopped
- 1 tbsp. ginger, grated
- 1 tbsp. garlic, minced
- 1 cup chickpeas
- 3 cups of water
- A pinch of salt and black pepper
- 14 ounces tomatoes, chopped
- 1 and ½ cups brown rice

Directions:

Melt the butter on Sauté. Add onion and cook for 7 minutes. Add salt, pepper, chana masala, ginger, and garlic. Cook for 1 minute more. Add tomatoes, chickpeas, rice, and water. Mix and cover. Cook on High for 20 minutes. Open and serve.

Wild Mushroom Rice
Cook time: 10 minutes |Serves: 6| Per serving: Calories 189; Carbs 9g; Fat 3g; Protein 8g

Ingredients:

- 1 and ½ cups Arborio rice
- 2 tbsps. butter
- 4 ounces wild mushrooms, roughly chopped
- 3 shallots, chopped
- 8 ounces cremini mushrooms, roughly chopped
- 2 cups veggie stock
- 1 tsp. fennel seeds
- A pinch of salt and black pepper
- 2 tbsps. parsley, chopped

Directions:

Melt the butter on Sauté. Add fennel seeds, rice, and shallots. Cook for 3 minutes. Add stock, mushrooms, and cover. Cook on High for 4 minutes. Open and press Sauté. Cook for 2 minutes and add parsley, salt, and pepper. Mix and serve.

Simple Black Rice
Cook time: 25 minutes |Serves: 6| Per serving: Calories 182; Carbs 18g; Fat 6g; Protein 4g

Ingredients:

- 2 ¾ cups water
- 1 tbsp. butter
- Salt and pepper to taste

- 2 cups black rice

Directions:

Melt the butter on Sauté. Add rice, season with salt and pepper, and cook for 3 minutes. Add water and cover the pot. Cook on High for 22 minutes. Serve.

Italian Rice Salad
Cook time: 7 minutes |Serves: 4| Per serving: Calories 170; Carbs 22g; Fat 6g; Protein 6g

Ingredients:

- 2 cups Arborio rice
- 4 cups of water
- A pinch of salt
- 1 tbsp. butter
- 2 tomatoes, sliced
- 1 cup black olives, pitted and sliced
- 1 bunch basil, chopped
- 3 tbsps. pickled capers, drained

Directions:

Melt the butter on Sauté and add rice. Cook for 2 minutes. Add water and cover the pot. Cook on High for 5 minutes. Strain rice and place it in a bowl. Add salt, tomatoes, capers, olives, basil, and mix well. Serve.

Lentils and Tomato Stew
Cook time: 19 minutes |Serves: 4| Per serving: Calories 212; Carbs 15g; Fat 6g; Protein 11g

Ingredients:

- 1 tbsp. butter
- 1 green bell pepper, chopped
- 1 yellow onion, chopped
- 1 celery stalk, chopped
- 1 tsp. curry powder
- 1 and ½ cups of lentils
- 2 cups of water
- 1 and ½ cups tomatoes, chopped
- Salt and black pepper to the taste

Directions:

Melt the butter on Sauté. Add onion, tomatoes, celery, and bell pepper. Mix and cook for 4 minutes. Add curry, salt, pepper, lentils, and water. Cover and cook on High for 15 minutes. Serve.

Lentil Soup
Cook time: 10 minutes |Serves: 8| Per serving: Calories 180; Carbs 26g; Fat 5g; Protein 10g

Ingredients:

- 8 cups of veggie stock
- 2 cups green lentils
- 1 and ½ pounds red potatoes, cubed
- 1 yellow onion, chopped
- 8 ounces mushrooms, cut in quarters
- 2 carrots, sliced
- Salt and pepper to the taste
- 2 celery ribs, chopped
- 2 bay leaves
- 4 garlic cloves, minced
- 2 tsps. thyme, dry
- 1 tbsp. soy sauce
- 1 tsp. rosemary, dry
- ½ tsp. sage, dry

Directions:

Add everything in the pot and cover. Cook on High for 10 minutes. Open and discard bay leaves. Serve.

Mushroom Lentil Burger
Cook time: 16 minutes |Serves: 4| Per serving: Calories 180; Carbs 20g; Fat 8g; Protein 13g

Ingredients:

- 1 cup mushrooms, chopped
- 2 tsps. ginger, grated
- 1 cup yellow onion, chopped
- 1 cup red lentils
- 1 sweet potato, chopped
- 2 and ½ cups veggie stock
- ¼ cup hemp seeds
- ¼ cup parsley, chopped
- 1 tbsp. curry powder
- ¼ cup cilantro, chopped
- 1 cup quick oats
- 4 tbsps. rice flour
- 2 tbsps. butter, divided

Directions:

Melt 1 butter on Sauté. Add onion, mushrooms, and ginger and cook for 2 minutes. Add lentils, stock, sweet potatoes, and cover. Cook on High for 6 minutes. Open and mash the potato with a potato masher. Add parsley, hemp, curry powder, cilantro, oats, and rice flour and stir well. Mix and transfer to a bowl. Make 8 patties. Clean the pot and melt the remaining butter. Cook the patties 3 to 4 minutes per side. Serve.

Pineapple Curry
Cook time: 36 minutes |Serves: 4| Per serving: Calories 371; Carbs 20g; Fat 6g; Protein 16g

Ingredients:

- 1 cup peas, soaked and drained
- 1 cup brown lentils
- 4 cups of water
- 3 tbsps. olive oil
- 1 yellow onion, chopped
- 1 tsp. curry powder
- ½ tsp. turmeric powder
- ¼ tsp. cinnamon powder
- ½ tsp. cumin, ground
- 1 cup canned pineapple, cut into medium chunks
- 2 tbsps. butter

Directions:

In the pot, mix peas with lentils. Add 3 ½ cups of water and cover. Cook on High for 25 minutes. Drain and transfer to a bowl. Add oil to the pot and heat on Sauté. Add cinnamon, turmeric, cumin, curry powder, and onions. Cook for 6 minutes. Return peas and lentils to the pot. Add butter, pineapple, and ½ cup water. Cover and cook on High for 5 minutes. Open and serve.

Chapter 7 Side Dishes

Orange Spiced Carrots

Cook time: 7 minutes |Serves: 6 | Per serving: Calories 187; Carbs 38g; Fat 4g; Protein 2g

Ingredients:

- 2 lbs. baby carrots, chopped
- 1/2 cup packed brown sugar
- 1/2 cup orange juice
- 2 tbsps. butter
- 3/4 tsp. ground cinnamon
- 1/2 tsp. salt
- 1/4 tsp. ground nutmeg
- 1 tbsp. cornstarch
- 1/4 cup cold water

Directions:

Combine the first seven ingredients in the pot. Cover and cook on Low for 3 minutes. Do a quick release and open. Press Sauté and bring it to a boil. Mix water and cornstarch in a bowl and add to the carrot mixture. Cook for 2 minutes. Serve.

Turnip Greens

Cook time: 5 minutes |Serves: 10| Per serving: Calories 63; Carbs 8 g; Fat 1g; Protein 2g

Ingredients:

- 2 lbs. peeled turnips, chopped
- 12 oz. fresh turnip greens
- 1 medium onion, chopped
- 2 tbsps. sugar
- Salt and pepper to taste
- 5 cups of broth

Directions:

Combine everything in the pot. Cover and cook on High for 5 minutes. Do a quick release and serve.

Lemon Red Potatoes

Cook time: 12 minutes |Serves: 6| Per serving: Calories 150; Carbs 18g; Fat 8g; Protein 2g

Ingredients:

- 1 1/2 lbs. medium red potatoes

- 1/4 cup water
- 1/4 cup butter, melted
- 3 tbsps. minced fresh parsley
- 1 tbsp. lemon juice
- 1 tbsp. minced chives
- Salt and pepper to taste

Directions:

Cut a strip of peel around the middle of each potato. Place potatoes and water in the Instant Pot. Cover and cook on High for 12 minutes. Do a quick release and open. Drain and return potatoes to the pot. Combine butter, parsley, lemon juice, and chives in a bowl. Pour over the potatoes and mix. Season with salt and pepper and serve.

Brussels Sprouts with Cranberries and Hazelnuts
Cook time: 3 minutes |Serves: 8 | Per serving: Calories 190; Carbs 20g; Fat 9g; Protein 4g

Ingredients:

- 2 lbs. fresh Brussels sprouts, sliced
- 2 large apples, chopped
- 1/3 cup dried cranberries
- 1/3 cup cider vinegar
- 1/4 cup maple syrup
- 2 tbsps. olive oil
- 1 tsp. salt
- 1/2 tsp. coarsely ground pepper
- 3/4 cup chopped hazelnuts, toasted

Directions:

Combine Brussels, apples, and cranberries in a bowl. Whisk vinegar, syrup, oil, salt, and pepper and pour over Brussels sprouts mixture. Mix well. Transfer everything to the pot. Cover and cook on High for 3 minutes. Do a quick release and open. Top with hazelnuts and serve.

Beet Salad
Cook time: 20 minutes |Serves: 8| Per serving: Calories 161; Carbs 24g; Fat 7g; Protein 3g

Ingredients:

- 6 medium fresh beets
- 1 1/2 cups water
- 1/4 cup extra virgin olive oil
- 3 tbsps. lemon juice
- 2 tbsps. cider vinegar

- 2 tbsps. honey
- 1/4 tsp. salt
- 1/4 tsp. pepper
- 2 large grapefruits, peeled and sectioned
- 2 small red onions, halved and sliced

Directions:

Scrub beets, trimming tops to 1 inch. Add the water to the Instant Pot and place a trivet. Place the beets on the trivet. Cover and cook on High for 20 minutes. Do a quick release and open. Whisk together the next six ingredients (starting from water) and pour over beets. Add onion and grapefruit. Mix and serve.

BBQ Baked Beans

Cook time: 35 minutes |Serves: 8| Per serving: Calories 190; Carbs 40g; Fat 1g; Protein 7g

Ingredients:

- 16 oz. dried great northern beans, soaked overnight, and drained
- 2 cups of water
- 1 medium onion, chopped
- 2 tsps. garlic powder, divided
- 2 tsps. onion powder, divided
- 1 cup barbecue sauce
- 3/4 cup packed brown sugar
- 1/2 tsp. ground nutmeg
- 1/4 tsp. ground cloves
- 2 tsps. hot pepper sauce

Directions:

In the pot, combine beans, water, onion, 1 tsp. garlic powder and 1 tsp. onion powder. Cover and cook on High for 30 minutes. Do a quick release and open. Stir in sauce, sugar, nutmeg, cloves, hot pepper sauce, and remaining garlic and onion powder. Close and cook on High for 3 minutes. Open and serve.

Summer Squash, and Zucchini with Cheese

Cook time: 2 minutes |Serves: 8 | Per serving: Calories 100; Carbs 10g; Fat 4g; Protein 4g

Ingredients:

- 1 lb. medium yellow summer squash, chopped
- 1 lb. medium zucchini, chopped
- 2 medium tomatoes, chopped
- 1 cup vegetable broth

- ¼ cup thinly sliced green onions
- ½ tsp. salt
- ¼ tsp. pepper
- 1 ½ cups Caesar salad croutons, coarsely crushed
- ½ cup shredded cheddar cheese

Directions:

Place the squash, tomatoes, broth, green onions, salt, and pepper to the Instant Pot. Cover and cook on High for 2 minutes. Open and serve topped with croutons, and cheese.

Steamed Leeks
Cook time: 5 minutes |Serves: 6| Per serving: Calories 83; Carbs 16g; Fat 2g; Protein 2g

Ingredients:

- 1 large tomato, chopped
- 1 small navel orange, chopped
- 2 tbsps. minced fresh parsley
- 2 tbsps. sliced olives
- 1 tsp. capers, drained
- 1 tsp. red wine vinegar
- 1 tsp. olive oil
- ½ tsp. grated orange zest
- ½ tsp. pepper
- 6 medium leeks (white portion only), halved lengthwise, cleaned
- Crumbled feta cheese for serving
- 1 cup water for the pot

Directions:

Combine the first 9 ingredients. Set aside. Place a trivet in the pot and add 1 cup of water. Place leeks on the trivet and close the pot. Cook on High for 2 minutes. Do a quick release and open. Transfer leeks to a platter. Spoon tomato mixture on top. Sprinkle with cheese and serve.

Spaghetti Squash with Tomatoes
Cook time: 10 minutes |Serves: 5 | Per serving: Calories 92; Carbs 15g; Fat 3g; Protein 3g

Ingredients:

- 1 medium spaghetti squash, halved lengthwise, seeds removed
- 1 can (14 oz.) diced tomatoes, drained
- ¼ cup sliced green olives with pimientos
- 1 tsp. dried oregano
- ½ tsp. salt

- ½ tsp. pepper
- ½ cup shredded cheddar cheese
- ¼ cup minced fresh basil
- 1 cup water for the pot

Directions:

Place a trivet in the pot and add 1 cup of water. Place squash on the trivet. Cover and cook on High for 7 minutes. Do a quick release and open. Remove squash and clean the pot. Use a fork to make spaghetti from the squash. Discard skin. Return squash to the pot. Add tomatoes, olives, oregano, salt, and pepper. Cook on Sauté for 3 minutes. Top with cheese and basil and serve.

Buffalo Wing Potatoes
Cook time: 5 minutes |Serves: 6 | Per serving: Calories 182; Carbs 32g; Fat 4g; Protein 6g

Ingredients:

- 2 lbs. Yukon Gold potatoes, cut into 1-in. cubes
- 1 small sweet yellow pepper, chopped
- ½ small red onion, chopped
- ¼ cup Buffalo wing sauce
- ½ cup shredded cheddar cheese
- Toppings: sliced green onions and sour cream
- 1 cup water for the pot

Directions:

Add water to the pot and place a steamer basket. Place potatoes, yellow pepper, and onion in the basket. Cover and cook on High for 3 minutes. Open and remove vegetables to a bowl. Clean the pot and place in the vegetables. Add the sauce and coat. Sprinkle the cheese and cover. Let stand for 2 minutes or until cheese melts. Top with sour cream and green onions and serve.

Mushroom Rice Pilaf
Cook time: 5 minutes |Serves: 6| Per serving: Calories 209; Carbs 30g; Fat 8g; Protein 4g

Ingredients:

- ¼ cup butter
- 1 cup medium-grain rice
- ½ lb. sliced baby portobello mushrooms
- 6 green onions, chopped
- 2 garlic cloves, minced
- 1 cup of water
- 4 tsps. better than bouillon vegetarian

Directions:

Melt the butter on Sauté in the Instant Pot. Add rice and cook for 5 minutes. Add garlic, green onions, and mushrooms. In a bowl, whisk the water and bouillon. Pour over rice mixture. Cover and cook on High for 4 minutes. Open and serve.

Rosemary Beets
Cook time: 20 minutes |Serves: 8| Per serving: Calories 200; Carbs 37g; Fat 4g; Protein 6g

Ingredients:

- 5 large fresh beets, scrubbed and trimmed
- 1 tbsp. olive oil
- 1 medium red onion, chopped
- 2 garlic cloves, minced
- 1 medium orange, peeled and chopped
- ⅓ cup honey
- ¼ cup white balsamic vinegar
- 1 tbsp. minced fresh rosemary
- 2 tsps. minced fresh thyme
- ¾ tsp. salt
- ½ tsp. Chinese five-spice powder
- ½ tsp. coarsely ground pepper
- 1 cup crumbled feta cheese
- 1 cup water for the pot

Directions:

Place the trivet and 1 cup water in the pot. Place the beets on the trivet and cover. Cook on High for 20 minutes. Open and remove beets. Clean the pot. Peel and cut beets into wedges. Heat the oil on Sauté. Cook onions for 5 minutes. Add garlic and cook for 1 minute more. Stir in honey, orange, vinegar, rosemary, thyme, salt, spice, pepper, and beets. Heat through and sprinkle with cheese. Serve.

Cooked Black-Eyed Peas
Cook time: 20 minutes |Serves: 8| Per serving: Calories 67; Carbs 11g; Fat 1g; Protein 4g

Ingredients:

- 16 oz. dried black-eyed peas
- 4 cups of water
- 1 medium onion, chopped
- 2 garlic cloves, chopped
- Season salt and pepper to taste
- Sliced green onions for garnish

Directions:

Rinse and sort the black-eyed peas. Place in the pot. Add water, onion, garlic, salt, and pepper. Cover and cook on High for 18 minutes. Open and sprinkle with green onions. Serve.

Cooked White Beans
Cook time: 30 minutes |Serves: 8| Per serving: Calories 167; Carbs 32g; Fat 2g; Protein 8g

Ingredients:

- 1 lb. dried great northern beans, soaked overnight
- 3 cans (14 ½ oz. each) reduced-sodium broth
- 1 ½ cups water
- 1 large onion, chopped
- 1 tbsp. onion powder
- 1 tbsp. garlic powder
- Pepper to taste
- Thinly sliced green onions, optional

Directions:

Place the beans, broth, water, onion, and seasonings in the pot. Cover and cook on High for 30 minutes. Do a quick release and open. Sprinkle with green onions and serve.

Delicious Basmati Rice with Veggies
Cook time: 6 minutes |Serves: 4| Per serving: Calories 242; Carbs 1g; Fat 3g; Protein 6g

Ingredients:

- 1 yellow bell pepper, chopped
- 1 tbsp. olive oil
- 1 yellow onion, chopped
- 1 carrot, grated
- 2 cups basmati rice
- 3 cups of water
- ½ cup peas
- A pinch of salt

Directions:

Heat oil on Sauté. Add onion and cook for 2 minutes. Add the rest of the ingredients and cover. Cook on High for 4 minutes. Open and serve.

Mixed Mash
Cook time: 5 minutes |Serves: 4| Per serving: Calories 247; Carbs 55g; Fat 1g; Protein 8g

Ingredients:

- 2 pounds potatoes, peeled and sliced

- 1 and ½ cups of water
- 8 ounces cauliflower florets
- 1 garlic clove, minced
- A pinch of salt

Directions:

In the pot, add potatoes, water, cauliflower, and salt. Mix and cover. Cook on High for 5 minutes. Open and add garlic. Mix and serve.

Sweet Potatoes Side Dish
Cook time: 10 minutes |Serves: 4| Per serving: Calories 210; Carbs 12g; Fat 4g; Protein 10g

Ingredients:

- 4 sweet potatoes, peeled and chopped
- 1 cup of water
- A pinch of salt and black pepper
- ¼ teaspoon cumin, ground
- A pinch of hot paprika

Directions:

Add water in the pot and add a steamer basket. Add potatoes on top. Cover and cook for 10 minutes on High. Divide potatoes on plates. Sprinkle with salt, pepper, cumin, and paprika and serve.

Cauliflower Rice
Cook time: 6 minutes |Serves: 4| Per serving: Calories 192; Carbs 9g; Fat 4g; Protein 7g

Ingredients:

- 2 tbsps. olive oil
- 1 cauliflower head, florets separated
- A pinch of salt and black pepper
- ½ tsp. parsley, dried
- ¼ tsp. cumin, ground
- ¼ tsp. paprika
- ¼ tsp. turmeric
- 1 cup of water
- Handful cilantro, chopped
- 1 tbsp. lemon juice

Directions:

Add the water to the pot and place in a steamer basket. Add cauliflower and cover. Cook on High for 2 minutes. Open and remove the cauliflower to a plate. Clean the pot, add oil and heat to Sauté.

Add cauliflower and blitz it into very fine grains. Add salt, pepper, parsley flakes, cumin, paprika, turmeric, lemon juice, and cilantro. Cook for 4 minutes. Serve.

Sweet Brussels Sprouts
Cook time: 5 minutes |Serves: 8 | Per serving: Calories 193; Carbs 8g; Fat 4g; Protein 10g

Ingredients:

- 2 pounds Brussels sprouts, trimmed
- 1 tbsp. olive oil
- 1 tsp. orange zest, grated
- ¼ cup orange juice
- 2 tbsps. stevia
- A pinch of salt and black pepper

Directions:

Heat oil in the pot on Sauté. Add sprouts and cook for 1 minute. Add orange zest, juice, stevia, salt, and pepper. Mix and cover. Cook on High for 4 minutes. Open and serve.

Simple Roasted Potatoes
Cook time: 15 minutes |Serves: 4| Per serving: Calories 190; Carbs 10g; Fat 6g; Protein 9g

Ingredients:

- 1 and ½ pounds potatoes, cut into wedges
- ¼ cup avocado oil
- A pinch of salt and black pepper
- ½ tsp. onion powder
- ¼ tsp. sweet paprika
- 1 cup veggie stock
- 1 tsp. garlic powder

Directions:

Heat oil on Sauté. Add potatoes and cook for 8 minutes. Add the remaining ingredients and mix. Cover and cook on High for 7 minutes. Serve.

Squash Risotto
Cook time: 12 minutes |Serves: 4| Per serving: Calories 231; Carbs 9g; Fat 5g; Protein 12g

Ingredients:

- ½ cup yellow onion
- 3 garlic cloves, minced
- 1 red bell pepper, chopped
- A drizzle of olive oil

- 1 and ½ cups Arborio rice
- 2 cups butternut squash, chopped
- 3 and ½ cups veggie stock
- 8 ounces mushrooms, chopped
- ½ tsp. coriander, ground
- A pinch of salt and black pepper
- ¼ tsp. oregano, dried
- 3 cups mixed spinach, kale, and chard
- 1 handful parsley, chopped

Directions:

Heat the oil on Sauté. Add onion, bell pepper, squash, and garlic. Cook for 5 minutes. Add rice, stock, mushrooms, salt, pepper, oregano, and coriander. Stir and cover. Cook on High for 5 minutes. Open and add parsley and mixed greens. Stir and cook on Sauté for 2 minutes. Serve.

Fried Cabbage
Cook time: 6 minutes |Serves: 4| Per serving: Calories 200; Carbs 8g; Fat 4g; Protein 5g

Ingredients:

- 1 cabbage head, sliced
- 1 yellow onion, chopped
- 2 tsps. stevia
- 2 tsps. balsamic vinegar
- 3 garlic cloves, minced
- 1 tbsp. olive oil
- A pinch of salt and black pepper
- 2 tsps. mustard

Directions:

Heat oil on Sauté. Add onion and garlic and cook for 2 minutes. Add cabbage, stevia, vinegar, mustard, salt, and pepper. Mix and cover. Cook on High for 4 minutes. Stir and serve.

Spanish Risotto
Cook time: 15 minutes |Serves: 6| Per serving: Calories 200; Carbs 6g; Fat 4g; Protein 8g

Ingredients:

- 1 cup yellow onion, chopped
- 3 tbsps. olive oil
- 2 cups white rice
- ¾ cup tomatoes, crushed
- 2 garlic cloves, minced

- 2 and ½ cups veggie stock
- ¼ cup cilantro, chopped
- ½ tsp. chili powder

Directions:

Heat oil on Sauté. Add onion and garlic and cook for 4 minutes. Add rice and cook for 2 minutes. Add stock, tomatoes, and chili powder. Stir and cover. Cook on High for 8 minutes. Add cilantro, salt, and pepper. Stir and serve.

Quinoa Side Dish

Cook time: 2 minutes |Serves: 4| Per serving: Calories 182; Carbs 8g; Fat 4g; Protein 10g

Ingredients:

- 2 cups quinoa
- 3 cups of water
- Juice of 1 lemon
- A pinch of salt and black pepper
- A handful of mixed parsley, cilantro, and basil, chopped

Directions:

In the pot, mix quinoa with water, lemon, salt, pepper, and mixed herbs. Stir and cover. Cook on High for 2 minutes. Leave quinoa aside for 10 minutes. Fluff and serve.

Beans Side Dish

Cook time: 30 minutes |Serves: 6| Per serving: Calories 261; Carbs 9g; Fat 5g; Protein 12g

Ingredients:

- 1 tsp. olive oil
- 16 ounces black beans, soaked overnight and drained
- 12 ounces green bell pepper, chopped
- 12 ounces sweet onion, chopped
- 4 garlic cloves, minced
- 2 and ½ tsp. cumin, ground
- 2 tbsps. tomato paste
- 1 tsp. stevia
- 2 quarts water
- A pinch of salt

Directions:

Heat oil on Sauté. Add onion and bell pepper and cook for 5 minutes. Add stevia, garlic, cumin, and tomato paste. Cook for 1 minute more. Add beans and water. Stir and cover. Cook on High for 25 minutes. Mash beans and mix. Add salt and mix. Serve.

Green Beans Side Dish
Cook time: 4 minutes |Serves: 6| Per serving: Calories 182; Carbs 6g; Fat 4g; Protein 8g

Ingredients:

- 1-pound green beans, trimmed
- 8 ounces white mushrooms, sliced
- 1 yellow onion, chopped
- 2 tbsps. olive oil
- ½ cup veggie stock
- 2 tbsps. flax meal
- A pinch of salt and black pepper

Directions:

Heat oil in the Instant Pot on Sauté. Add onion and cook for 1 minute. Add half of the stock and mushrooms. Mix and cook for 1 minute. Add rest of the stock, green beans, salt, pepper, and flax meal. Mix and cover. Cook on High for 2 minutes. Serve.

Fried Rice
Cook time: 20 minutes |Serves: 4| Per serving: Calories 261; Carbs 10g; Fat 6g; Protein 6g

Ingredients:

- ¼ cup olive oil
- 1 cup basmati rice
- 1 and ½ cups of water
- ½ sweet onion, chopped
- ½ cup carrots, chopped
- ½ cup green peas
- 1 teaspoon sesame oil
- Coconut aminos to taste
- 1 teaspoon garlic powder

Directions:

In the pot, mix water with rice. Stir and cover. Cook on High for 12 minutes. Add oil, carrots, onions, green peas, garlic powder, and coconut aminos. Stir and cover. Cook for 6 minutes more. Stir and drizzle with sesame oil. Serve.

Caramelized Sweet Potatoes
Cook time: 20 minutes |Serves: 2 | Per serving: Calories 182; Carbs 9g; Fat 5g; Protein 9g

Ingredients:

- 2 tbsps. coconut oil
- 2 sweet potatoes, scrubbed
- 1 cup of water
- A pinch of salt and black pepper
- A pinch of chili powder

Directions:

Add water to the Instant Pot and place the steamer basket at the bottom. Add sweet potatoes. Cover and cook on High for 15 minutes. Remove and slice the potatoes. Clean the pot and press Sauté. Heat oil and add the sliced sweet potatoes. Season with salt, pepper, and chili powder and brown for 2 minutes on each side. Serve.

Thai Coconut Rice
Cook time: 3 minutes |Serves: 4| Per serving: Calories 211; Carbs 6g; Fat 5g; Protein 12g

Ingredients:

- 14 ounces milk
- 1 and ½ cups jasmine rice
- 1 tbsp. cream
- 2 tsps. sugar
- ½ cup of water
- A pinch of salt
- Coconut flakes, toasted for serving

Directions:

In the pot, mix rice, water, milk, cream, sugar, and a pinch of salt. Cover and cook on High for 3 minutes. Stir rice and divide between plates. Sprinkle with coconut flakes and serve.

Broccoli and Garlic
Cook time: 12 minutes |Serves: 4| Per serving: Calories 182; Carbs 6g; Fat 4g; Protein 6g

Ingredients:

- 6 garlic cloves, minced
- 1 broccoli head, florets separated
- ½ cup of water
- 1 tbsp. olive oil
- 1 tbsp. rice wine
- A pinch of salt and black pepper

Directions:

Add the water to the pot and place a steamer basket. Add broccoli and cover. Cook on High for 10 minutes. Submerge broccoli in cold water for a few minutes. Then drain and put it in another bowl. Clean the pot, press Sauté, and add the oil. Stir and cook for 1 minute. Add broccoli, salt, pepper, and rice wine. Stir and cover. Cook on High for 1 minute. Serve.

Chapter 8 Drinks

Zobo Drink
Cook time: 10 minutes |Serves: 8| Per serving: Calories 65; Carbs 7g; Fat 2.6g; Protein 1.14g

Ingredients:

- 2 cups dried hibiscus petals (zobo leaves), rinsed
- Pineapple rind from 1 pineapple
- 1 cup of granulated sugar
- 1 tsp. fresh ginger, grated
- 10 cups of water

Directions:

Add water, ginger, and sugar into the pot and mix well. Then add zobo leaves and pineapple rind. Cover and cook on High for 10 minutes. Open and discard solids. Chill and serve.

Basil Lime Green Tea
Cook time: 4 minutes |Serves: 8| Per serving: Calories 32; Carbs 8g; Fat 0g; Protein 0g

Ingredients:

- 8 cups of filtered water
- 10 bags of green tea
- ¼ cup of honey
- A pinch of baking soda
- Lime slices to taste
- Lemon slices to taste
- Basil leaves to taste

Directions:

Add water, honey, and baking soda in the pot and mix. Add the tea bags and cover. Cook on High for 4 minutes. Open and serve with lime slices, lemon slices, and basil leaves.

Turmeric Coconut Milk
Cook time: 15 minutes |Serves: 8| Per serving: Calories 42; Carbs 9g; Fat 0g; Protein 0g

Ingredients:

- 13.5 oz. coconut milk
- 3 cups of filtered water
- 2 tsps. turmeric powder
- 3 whole cloves
- 2 cinnamon sticks

- ½ tsp. ginger powder
- A pinch of pepper
- 2 tbsp. honey

Directions:

Place everything except the honey in the pot. Cover and cook on High for 15 minutes. Remove cloves and cinnamon sticks. Add honey, mix and serve.

Berry Lemonade Tea

Cook time: 12 minutes |Serves: 4| Per serving: Calories 21; Carbs 8g; Fat 0.2g; Protein 0.4g

Ingredients:

- 3 tea bags
- 2 cups of natural lemonade
- 1 cup of frozen mixed berries
- 2 cups of water
- 1 lemon, sliced

Directions:

Put everything in the Instant Pot and cover. Cook on High for 12 minutes. Open, strain, and serve.

Swedish Glögg

Cook time: 15 minutes |Serves: 1 | Per serving: Calories 194; Carbs 41g; Fat 3g; Protein 1.7g

Ingredients:

- ½ cup of orange juice
- ½ cup of water
- 1 piece of ginger cut into ½ pieces
- 1 whole clove
- 1 opened cardamom pods
- 2 tbsps. orange zest
- 1 cinnamon stick
- 1 whole allspice
- 1 vanilla bean

Directions:

Add everything in the pot. Cover and cook on High for 15 minutes. Open and serve.

Blackberry Drink

Cook time: 10 minutes |Serves: 4| Per serving: Calories 223; Carbs 58g; Fat 0.4g; Protein 1.2g

Ingredients:

- 2 cups blackberries
- 2 cups of water
- 1 cup of sugar
- 1 lemon, sliced

Directions:

Put everything in the pot except for the lemon. Cover and cook on High for 10 minutes. Open and serve with lemon slices.

Spiced Cider
Cook time: 10 minutes |Serves: 3| Per serving: Calories 162; Carbs 41g; Fat 0.6g; Protein 1.3g

Ingredients:

- 3 apples, sliced
- 1 orange, sliced
- ¼ tsp. nutmeg
- ½ cup fresh cranberries
- 2 cinnamon sticks
- 3 cups of water
- 3 tbsps. cassava syrup

Directions:

Put everything in the pot and cover. Cook on High for 10 minutes. Open, strain, and serve.

Berry Kombucha
Cook time: 8 minutes |Serves: 6| Per serving: Calories 31; Carbs 7g; Fat 0.1g; Protein 0.2g

Ingredients:

- 4 cups sparkling water
- 1 cup of frozen mixed berries
- 4 cups kombucha

Directions:

Put everything in the pot and cover. Cook on High for 8 minutes. Open and serve.

Ginger Lemon Tea
Cook time: 15 minutes |Serves: 4| Per serving: Calories 27; Carbs 3.5g; Fat 0.7g; Protein 1.2g

Ingredients:

- 3 cups of water
- 1 (1-inch) piece fresh ginger, peeled

- 1 cup fresh lemon juice
- 1 tsp. ginger powder
- 1 tbsp. fenugreek seeds

Directions:

Put everything in the pot and cover. Cook on High for 15 minutes. Open, strain, and serve.

Spiced Ginger Cider

Cook time: 13 minutes |Serves: 12| Per serving: Calories 141; Carbs 35.2g; Fat 0.6g; Protein 0.4g

Ingredients:

- 2 small apples, peeled
- 12 cups apple cider
- 2 whole allspice
- 2 tsps. fresh ginger
- 4 tsps. orange zest
- 2 tsps. cinnamon powder
- 4 whole cloves
- ½ tsp. ground nutmeg

Directions:

Put everything in the pot. Cover and cook on High for 13 minutes. Open, strain, and serve.

Hot Chocolate

Cook time: 1 minute |Serves: 2| Per serving: Calories 60; Carbs 14g; Fat 3g; Protein 3g

Ingredients:

- 14 oz milk
- 2 tbsps. cocoa powder
- 3 tbsps. chocolate chips
- 2 tbsps. sweetener of choice

Directions:

Add everything in the pot. Cover and cook on High for 1 minute. Open, whisk and serve.

Sweet Rice Drink

Cook time: 4 minutes |Serves: 4| Per serving: Calories 92; Carbs 21g; Fat 3g; Protein 0g

Ingredients:

- 32 oz unsweetened rice milk
- 6 tbsps sugar

- 1 cinnamon stick broken into small chunks
- ¼ tsp vanilla extract
- Cinnamon powder for garnish

Directions:

Mix everything in the pot. Cover and cook on High for 4 minutes. Open, strain, and serve.

Creamy Eggnog
Cook time: 90 minutes |Serves: 8| Per serving: Calories 253; Carbs 20g; Fat 16g; Protein 6g

Ingredients:

- 6 eggs
- 2/3 cup sugar
- 2 cups whole milk
- 1 cup heavy cream
- ½ tsp vanilla extract
- ½ tsp nutmeg
- ¼ tsp salt
- Cinnamon powder for garnish

Directions:

Place a trivet in the pot and pour 5 cups of water. Press Sauté and bring it to a boil. Blend the eggs in a blender. Then add sugar and blend until mixed. Add milk, vanilla, cream, nutmeg, and salt. Blend to mix. Pour this mixture into a Pyrex dish and place it on top of the trivet. Set the Instant Pot on the "Slow Cooker" mode and adjust the time to 90 minutes. Cover with a glass lid. Do not lock the lid. Stir periodically until the eggnog thickens. Cool in the refrigerator and serve.

Brown Rice Horchata
Cook time: 10 minutes |Serves: 6| Per serving: Calories 145; Carbs 15g; Fat 2g; Protein 4g

Ingredients:

- 2 whole cinnamon sticks
- ¼ cup of brown rice
- 4 cups of water
- ¼ cup of raw almonds
- ½ cup of sugar

Directions:

Add the water, rice, almonds, and cinnamon to the Instant Pot. Cover and cook on High for 10 minutes. Open and remove the cinnamon sticks. Add the sugar and mix. Strain and serve.

Masala Chai

Cook time: 4 minutes |Serves: 2| Per serving: Calories 63; Carbs 11.6g; Fat 1.7g; Protein 2.4g

Ingredients:

- 3 sticks cinnamon
- 1/2 tsp. fennel seeds
- 1/2 cup milk
- 2 tsps. sugar
- 4 cardamom pods
- 4 thin slices of ginger
- 2 teabags
- 1.5 cups water
- 2 whole cloves

Directions:

Put everything in the pot and cover. Cook on High for 4 minutes. Open, Strain, and serve.

Chapter 9 Desserts

Egg Custard

Cook time: 30 minutes |Serves: 8| Per serving: Calories 155; Carbs 22.1g; Fat 5.1g; Protein 7g

Ingredients:

- 6 eggs
- 24-ounces of milk
- ½ cup honey
- ¼ tsp. ground cinnamon
- ¼ tsp. ground cardamom
- 1/8 tsp. ground allspice
- ¼ tsp. ground ginger
- ¼ tsp. ground nutmeg
- 1/8 tsp. ground cloves
- Salt, to taste
- 1 ½ cups water for the pot

Directions:

Whisk eggs with all the other ingredients and divide evenly into 8 ramekins. Place the trivet in the pot and add water. Cover and cook on Low for 30 minutes. Open and serve.

Sweet Potato Dessert Risotto

Cook time: 16 minutes |Serves: 6| Per serving: Calories 291; Carbs 42.5g; Fat 12.4g; Protein 5.5g

Ingredients:

- ½ cup risotto rice
- ½ cup milk
- 1 tbsp. butter
- ¾ cup of water
- ½ tsp. vanilla extract
- ½ tsp. cardamom powder
- ½ cup raisins
- ½ cup evaporated milk
- ¼ cup honey
- ½ tsp. cinnamon powder
- ½ tsp. salt
- 1 sweet potato, grated
- ½ cup almonds, roasted and grated

Directions:

Melt the butter on Sauté. Add the evaporated milk, milk, honey, and water. Mix and add cardamom, cinnamon, vanilla, and salt. Add rice and grated sweet potato. Cover and cook on High for 12 minutes. Open and add raisins. Simmer for 4 minutes. Top with almonds and serve.

Red Wine Poached Pears

Cook time: 18 minutes |Serves: 3| Per serving: Calories 434; Carbs 101.1g; Fat 0.38g; Protein 1.2g

Ingredients:

- 3 firm pears, peeled and stem attached
- ½ bottle red wine
- 2 cloves
- ½ tsp. ginger, grated
- ½ cinnamon, grated
- 1 bay laurel leaf
- 1 cup granulated sugar

Directions:

Put everything in the pot and cover. Cook on High for 8 minutes. Open and remove the pears. Simmer the mixture for 10 minutes on Sauté to thicken. Drizzle the red wine sauce on pears and serve.

Coconut Chocolate Fondue

Cook time: 3 minutes |Serves: 4| Per serving: Calories 266; Carbs 16.8g; Fat 21.4g; Protein 2.7g

Ingredients:

- 1 cup Swiss bittersweet chocolate (70%)
- 1 cup coconut cream
- 2 tsps. coconut milk powder
- 2 tsps. sugar
- 2 tsps. coconut essence
- 2 cups of water

Directions:

Mix chocolate, sugar, and coconut cream in a ceramic bowl. Arrange the trivet in the pot and add water. Place the bowl on the trivet and cover the pot. Cook on High for 3 minutes. Open and add essence and milk powder. Stir and serve.

Strawberry Rhubarb Tarts

Cook time: 5 minutes |Serves: 12 | Per serving: Calories 163; Carbs 26.2g; Fat 6.2g; Protein 1.6g

Ingredients:

- 1 cup of water
- 1-pound rhubarb, cut into ½ inch pieces
- ½ pound strawberries
- ¼ cup crystallized ginger, chopped
- Readymade 12 tart shells, short crust
- ½ cup honey
- ½ cup whipped cream

Directions:

Put everything in the pot except the tart shells and whipped cream. Cover and cook 5 minutes at High. Open and fill the tart shells with this mixture. Top with whipped cream and serve.

Hazelnut Flan

Cook time: 8 minutes |Serves: 10 | Per serving: Calories 244; Carbs 21.4g; Fat 14.2g; Protein 8.5g

Ingredients:

- 6 eggs
- ½ cups granulated sugar
- 4 cups whole milk
- 2 tsps. vanilla extract
- 4 egg yolks
- ¼ tsp. salt
- 1 cup whipping cream
- 8 tbsps. hazelnut syrup
- ½ cup caramel
- 2 cups of water

Directions:

Whisk together eggs, egg yolks, salt, and sugar in a bowl. Boil milk and add gradually to the egg mixture. Add vanilla extract, whipping cream, and hazelnuts syrup to the mixture. Put the caramel in the custard cups and add the hazelnut mixture in them. Arrange the trivet in the pot and add water. Place the custard cups on the trivet and cover the pot. Cook on High for 8 minutes. Open and cool. Keep in the refrigerator for 3 hours and serve.

Peanut Butter Custard

Cook time: 10 minutes |Serves: 10| Per serving: Calories 276; Carbs 21.9g; Fat 17.3g; Protein 10.1g

Ingredients:

- 1 cup caramel
- 4 whole eggs
- 4 egg yolks

- ½ cup granulated sugar
- ¼ tsp. salt
- 4 cups whole milk
- 1 cup whipping cream
- 2 tsps. vanilla extract
- 8 tbsps. peanut butter
- 2 cups of water

Directions:

Whisk together eggs, egg yolks, salt, and sugar in a bowl. Boil the milk and add gradually to the egg mixture. Add vanilla extract, whipping cream, and peanut butter to this mixture. Put the caramel in the custard cups and add the peanut butter mixture in them. Arrange the trivet in the pot and add water. Place custard cups on the trivet and cover. Cook on High for 10 minutes. Open and cool. Refrigerate for 3 hours and serve.

Cranberry Apple Rice Pudding

Cook time: 12 minutes |Serves: 4| Per serving: Calories 317; Carbs 5.9g; Fat 8.5g; Protein 6.2g

Ingredients:

- ¾ cup Arborio rice, soaked
- 2 pinches salt
- ¼ cup brown sugar
- 1½ cups milk
- 1½ tbsps. almonds, roasted and sliced, for garnish
- 1 tbsp. butter
- 1 apple, diced
- ¾ tsp. cinnamon powder
- ½ cup apple juice
- ¼ cup dried cranberries, for garnish
- ¼ cup whipped cream, for garnish

Directions:

Put the butter and rice in the pot and press Sauté. Cook for 4 minutes. Add everything except for the garnishes. Cover and cook on High for 8 minutes. Open and serve.

Chocolate Pudding

Cook time: 20 minutes |Serves: 6| Per serving: Calories 287; Carbs 31.9g; Fat 16.3g; Protein 4.2g

Ingredients:

- 2 tbsps. dark chocolate, grated
- 1/2 cup golden castor sugar

- 1 tsp. vanilla extract
- 1 tbsp. cocoa powder
- 1/2 cup butter
- 2 eggs
- 1/2 cup self-rising flour
- 2 cups of water

Directions:

Mix butter, sugar, eggs, and vanilla in a bowl. Add flour, chocolate, and cocoa powder in the egg mixture. Arrange the trivet in the pot and add the water. Place the bowl on the trivet and cover the pot. Cook on Low for 20 minutes. Open and cool the pudding in the refrigerator. Serve.

White Chocolate Orange Fondue
Cook time: 4 minutes |Serves: 6| Per serving: Calories 379; Carbs 38g; Fat 22.6g; Protein 3.8g

Ingredients:

- 1 cup Swiss white chocolate
- 1 cup fresh cream
- 2½ tsps. candied orange peel, chopped finely
- 2½ tsps. sugar
- 2½ tsps. orange essence
- 2½ cups water

Directions:

Mix white chocolate, sugar, and cream in a bowl. Arrange the trivet in the pot and add water. Place the bowl on the trivet and cover the pot. Cook on High for 4 minutes. Open and add orange peel and orange essence. Mix and serve.

Chocolate Hazelnut Lava Cake
Cook time: 10 minutes |Serves: 4| Per serving: Calories 355; Carbs 44.4g; Fat 19.3g; Protein 6.4g

Ingredients:

- ½ cup all-purpose flour
- ¼ cup hazelnut paste
- 2 tbsps. fresh cream
- ½ cup of sugar
- 1 pinch salt
- 4 tbsps. bitter cocoa powder
- ½ tsp. baking powder
- 1 egg
- ¾ cup milk

- ¼ cup olive oil
- 1 cup of water

Directions:

Mix flour, sugar, salt, baking powder, and cocoa powder in a bowl. Add egg, oil, milk and whisk well. Put this mixture into 4 ramekins and put hazelnut paste in the center. Arrange the trivet in the pot and add the water. Place the ramekins on the trivet and cover the pot. Cook on High for 10 minutes. Open and serve.

Pear and Apple Clafoutis
Cook time: 20 minutes |Serves: 8| Per serving: Calories 254; Carbs 53.3g; Fat 2.1g; Protein 5.8g

Ingredients:

- 2 eggs
- 1 cup apples, chopped
- 1 cup pears, chopped
- ¾ cup of sugar
- 2 cups all-purpose flour
- 1 cup milk
- 1 tbsp. vanilla extract
- 2 tbsps. powdered sugar
- 2 cups of water
- Butter, for greasing

Directions:

Grease a baking tin with butter. Mix together eggs, vanilla, and sugar in a bowl. Add milk, and flour gradually and pour in the tin. Top with chopped fruits and cover tightly with foil. Arrange the trivet in the pot and add water. Place the tin on the trivet and cover the pot. Cook on High for 20 minutes. Open and serve.

Almond and Cardamom Tapioca Pudding
Cook time: 8 minutes |Serves: 4| Per serving: Calories 245; Carbs 41g; Fat 7.9g; Protein 4.5g

Ingredients:

- 1/4 cup tapioca pearls
- ½ cup of water
- ½ tsp. cardamom powder
- 1 cup whole milk
- ½ cup of sugar
- ½ cup almonds, roasted
- 2 cups water for the pot

Directions:

Mix tapioca pearls, milk, sugar, cardamom, and water in a bowl. Arrange the trivet in the pot and add 2 cups of water. Place the bowl on the trivet and cover the pot. Cook on High for 8 minutes. Open and garnish with almonds. Serve.

Rice Pudding
Cook time: 20 minutes |Serves: 4| Per serving: Calories 236; Carbs 43g; Fat 4g; Protein 7g

Ingredients:

- 2 cups of whole milk
- 1 cup of long-grain rice
- ½ tsp. of grated nutmeg
- 1 tsp. vanilla extract
- 1 tsp. cinnamon
- 1 can (14 oz) condensed milk
- 1 ¼ cups of water
- A pinch of salt

Directions:

Rinse and drain the rice. Add the water, milk, cinnamon, nutmeg, and salt in the pot. Add rice and mix. Cover and cook on High for 20 minutes. Open and add the vanilla and sweetened condensed milk. Mix and serve.

Quinoa Pudding
Cook time: 45 minutes |Serves: 2| Per serving: Calories 400; Carbs 64.4g; Fat 18g; Protein 20g

Ingredients:

- 2 tbsps. ground almonds
- ¼ cup condensed milk
- Ground cardamom to taste
- 2 tsps. butter
- ½ cup quinoa
- 2 ½ cups milk

Directions:

Melt the butter on Sauté. Add the quinoa and cook for 2 minutes. Pour in the milk and bring to a boil. Continue to stir. Cover and cook on High for 10 minutes. Open and mix in the condensed milk, ground almonds, and cardamom. Cover and cook on Low for 30 minutes. Open and serve.

Mango Cheesecake
Cook time: 50 minutes |Serves: 8| Per serving: Calories 489; Carbs 42g; Fat 33g; Protein 6g

Ingredients:

- ½ cup of unsalted butter and 1 tbsp. unsalted butter at room temperature
- 2 minced mangos and 1 thinly sliced mango
- 16 ounces cream cheese
- ½ cup of sugar and 2 tbsps. sugar (divided)
- 2 cups of water and 2 tbsps. water (divided)
- 1 ½ cups of graham cracker crumbs
- 2 tbsps. cornstarch

Directions:

Mix the graham cracker crumbs, melted butter, and 2 tbsps. sugar in a bowl. Reserve 2 tbsps. of this mixture for the garnish. Grease a springform pan with butter. Add the crumb mixture to the pan and evenly press it down. Put it in the freezer for 15 minutes. Meanwhile, in a blender, combine the 2 chopped mangoes and 2 tbsps. of water. Puree until smooth. Beat cream cheese in a bowl until fluffy. Add the remaining 2 cups of sugar. Mix well. Add the cornstarch and mango puree and gently fold the mixture until mixed. Remove the pan from the freezer and pour the filling on top of the crust. Cover the pan with foil. Pour 2 cups water in the pot and place the trivet. Place the pan on top of the trivet and cover the pot. Cook on High for 50 minutes. Open and remove the foil. Cool at room temperature. Then cover with foil again and chill in the refrigerator for 6 hours. Serve.

Crème Brûlée

Cook time: 10 minutes |Serves: 1| Per serving: Calories 380; Carbs 12g; Fat 33.6g; Protein 3g

Ingredients:

- 1 tsp. raw sugar and 1 tsp. for topping
- 1 tsp. vanilla extract
- 1/3 cup of heavy cream
- A pinch lavender buds (before and after baking)
- A pinch of vanilla bean seeds
- 1 egg yolk
- 1 cup water for the pot

Directions:

Put 1 tsp. sugar in warm heavy cream and cool to room temperature. Whisk egg yolk into the cream mixture. Add vanilla bean seeds, vanilla extract, and lavender buds. Mix well and pour into a ramekin. Place the trivet into the pot and add 1 cup of water. Place the ramekin on the trivet and cover. Cook on High for 9 minutes. Open and cool. Then chill in the refrigerator. Sprinkle tsp. sugar and melt with a blow torch. Serve.

Apple Pear Crisp

Cook time: 10 minutes |Serves: 4 Per serving: Calories 291; Carbs 49g; Fat 9g; Protein 3.5g

Ingredients:

- 3 tbsps. butter, melted
- 1 tsp. ground cinnamon
- ½ cup of packed brown sugar
- ½ cup of all-purpose flour
- ½ cup of old-fashioned rolled oats
- ½ tsp. freshly grated nutmeg
- 2 peeled and sliced apples
- 2 peeled and sliced pears
- ½ cup of water

Directions:

In a bowl, mix the brown sugar, butter, oats, flour, cinnamon, and nutmeg. Evenly layer the apples and pears in the pot. Then evenly spread the oat mixture on top and pour the water on top of the oat mixture. Cover and cook on High for 5 minutes. Open and cook on Sauté until bubbles. Serve.

Brownies
Cook time: 35 minutes |Serves: 6| Per serving: Calories 238; Carbs 35g; Fat 9g; Protein 4.3g

Ingredients:

- ¾ cup of confectioners' sugar
- 1 cup of flour
- ¼ cup of cocoa powder
- 1 tsp. baking powder
- ½ tsp. baking soda
- ¼ cup of plain Greek yogurt
- 3 tbsps. plus 1 tsp. oil
- 2 tsps. salt
- 2 cups of water
- ½ cup of milk

Directions:

In a bowl, sift together the cocoa powder, flour, and sugar. Then place in the baking powder and baking soda. Mix well. Whisk the milk, yogurt, and 3 tbsps. of oil in another bowl. Mix the 2 mixtures and form a smooth batter. Grease a pan with the remaining oil. Pour the batter in it. Cover with aluminum foil. Pour the water in the pot and place in a trivet. Place the pan on the trivet and cover the pot. Cook on High for 35 minutes. Open the pot and remove the pan. Remove the foil and sprinkle with salt. Cool and serve.

Pumpkin Pie Pudding
Cook time: 20 minutes |Serves: 4| Per serving: Calories 194; Carbs 9g; Fat 16g; Protein 3.5g

Ingredients:

- 15 oz pumpkin purée
- ½ cup of heavy whipping cream
- ¾ cup of sugar
- 1 tsp. pumpkin pie spice
- 1 tsp. vanilla
- 2 eggs
- 1 ½ cups water for the pot

Directions:

Whisk 2 eggs and add all the remaining ingredients. Pour the water in the pot and place a trivet. Grease a baking pan and pour the mixture in it. Cover the pan with foil and place the pan on the trivet. Cover the pot and cook on High for 20 minutes. Open and serve.

Mango Jam
Cook time: 10 minutes |Serves: 8| Per serving: Calories 150; Carbs 16g; Fat 2g; Protein 3g

Ingredients:

- 1 and ½ pounds mango, peeled and cubed
- 1 tsp. nigella seeds
- Sugar to taste
- ½ cup apple cider vinegar
- 1-inch ginger, grated
- 1 cinnamon stick
- 4 cardamom pods
- 4 cloves

Directions:

Mix everything in the pot. Cover and cook on High for 10 minutes. Stir again and discard the cinnamon stick. Serve.

Lemon Pudding
Cook time: 5 minutes |Serves: 7| Per serving: Calories 121; Carbs 6g; Fat 3g; Protein 4g

Ingredients:

- 3 cups of milk
- Juice from 2 lemons
- Lemon zest from 2 lemons, grated
- ½ cup maple syrup
- 3 tbsps. coconut oil
- 3 tbsps. flax meal mixed with 6 tbsp. water

- 4 drops lemon oil
- 2 tbsps. agar agar
- 1 cup of water

Directions:

In the blender, mix milk, with lemon juice, lemon zest, maple syrup, oil, flax meal, lemon oil, agar-agar, and pulse well. Divide into 7 small jars and cover with lids. Add water to the pot and place a trivet. Arrange jars on the trivet. Cover and cook on High for 5 minutes. Serve.

Fruit Pie
Cook time: 10 minutes |Serves: 4| Per serving: Calories 152; Carbs 14g; Fat 4g; Protein 7g

Ingredients:

- 1 plum, chopped
- 1 pear, chopped
- 1 apple, chopped
- 2 tbsps. sugar
- 1 cup of water
- ¼ cup coconut, shredded
- ½ tsp. cinnamon powder
- 3 tbsp. coconut oil
- ¼ cup pecans, chopped

Directions:

Put the plum, apple, and pear in a bowl. Add oil, coconut, cinnamon, and sugar, and mix. Add water to the pot and place a trivet. Place the bowl on top. Cover and cook on High for 10 minutes. Top with pecans and serve.

Banana Cake
Cook time: 1 hour |Serves: 4| Per serving: Calories 326; Carbs 55g; Fat 16g; Protein 8g

Ingredients:

- 1 cup water
- ½ cup of sugar, powdered
- 2 cups coconut flour
- 3 bananas, peeled and mashed
- 2 tbsps. flax meal mixed with 4 tbsps. water
- 2 tsps. baking powder
- 1 tsp. cinnamon powder
- 1 tsp. nutmeg powder
- 1 tbsp. butter plus more for greasing

Directions:

In a bowl, mix the flax meal with sugar, baking powder, cinnamon, nutmeg, banana, butter, and flour. Mix and pour in a greased cake pan and cover with tin foil. Add the water to the pot and place in a trivet. Place the cake pan on top. Cover the pot and cook on High for 1 hour. Open, slice, and serve.

Molten Mocha Cake

Cook time: 25 minutes |Serves: 6| Per serving: Calories 423; Carbs 77g; Fat 25g; Protein 12g

Ingredients:

- 1 cup of water
- 4 large eggs
- 1 1/2 cups sugar
- 1/2 cup butter, melted
- 1 tbsp. vanilla extract
- 1 cup all-purpose flour
- 1/2 cup baking cocoa
- 1 tbsp. instant coffee granules
- 1/4 tsp. salt

Directions:

Pour water into the pot and place in a trivet. In a bowl, beat eggs, sugar, butter, and vanilla until mixed. In another bowl, whisk flour, cocoa, granules, and salt. Gradually beat into the egg mixture. Transfer to a greased baking dish. Cover loosely with foil and place on the trivet. Cover the pot and cook on High for 25 minutes. Open and serve.

Apple Comfort

Cook time: 12 minutes |Serves: 8| Per serving: Calories 433; Carbs 53g; Fat 24g; Protein 5g

Ingredients:

- 1 cup of water
- 6 medium tart apples, peeled and sliced
- 1 cup of sugar
- 1/4 cup all-purpose flour
- 2 tsps. ground cinnamon
- 2 large eggs
- 1 cup heavy whipping cream
- 1 tsp. vanilla extract
- 1 cup graham cracker crumbs
- 1/2 cup chopped pecans
- 1/4 cup butter, melted

- Vanilla ice cream, for serving

Directions:

Add water to the pot and place in a trivet. In a bowl, combine apples, sugar, flour, and cinnamon. Spoon into a greased baking dish. In a small bowl, whisk eggs, cream, and vanilla. Pour over apple mixture. In another bowl, combine cracker crumbs, pecans, and butter. Sprinkle over the top. Loosely cover the dish with foil and place it on the trivet. Cover the pot and cook on High for 12 minutes. Open and serve with ice cream.

Black and Blue Cobbler
Cook time: 15 minutes |Serves: 6| Per serving: Calories 391; Carbs 80g; Fat 7g; Protein 5g

Ingredients:

- 1 3/4 cups of water, divided
- 1 cup all-purpose flour
- 1 1/2 cups of sugar, divided
- 1 tsp. baking powder
- 1/4 tsp. salt
- 1/4 tsp. ground cinnamon
- 1/4 tsp. ground nutmeg
- 2 eggs, lightly beaten
- 2 tbsps. of whole milk
- 2 tbsps. of oil
- 2 cups fresh or frozen blackberries
- 2 cups fresh or frozen blueberries
- 1 tsp. grated orange zest
- Whipped cream or vanilla ice cream, for serving

Directions:

Add 1 cup of water in the pot and place in a trivet. In a bowl, combine flour, ¾ cup sugar, baking powder, salt, cinnamon, and nutmeg. In another bowl, combine the eggs, milk, and oil. Stir into dry ingredients just until moistened. Pour batter in a greased baking dish. In a pan, combine the berries, remaining water, orange zest, and remaining sugar and bring to a boil. Immediately pour over batter. Cover the baking pan with foil and place it on the trivet. Cover the pot and cook on High for 15 minutes. Open and uncover the baking pan. Cool for 30 minutes and serve with whipped cream or ice cream.

Pumpkin Flans
Cook time: 35 minutes |Serves: 6| Per serving: Calories 235; Carbs 45g; Fat 3g; Protein 9g

Ingredients:

- 1 cup of sugar, divided
- ¼ cups of water
- 1 ½ cups of fat-free evaporated milk
- 3 eggs
- 1 egg white
- ¼ tsp. salt
- ¼ tsp. each ground ginger, cinnamon, and cloves
- 1 cup canned pumpkin
- 1 tsp. vanilla extract

Directions:

In the Instant Pot, combine 1/3 of a cup of sugar, and ¼ a cup of water. Cook and stir until sugar begins to melt. Cook without stirring until amber, about 20 minutes. Quickly pour into 6 ungreased ramekins. Coat the bottoms. Set aside for 10 minutes. In a saucepan, heat milk until bubbles form. In a bowl, whisk eggs, egg white, salt, spices, and remaining 2/3 of a cup of sugar and blend. Slowly stir in hot milk. Stir in vanilla and pumpkin. Pour into ramekins. Cover each ramekin with foil. Clean the pot and 1 cup water and a trivet. Place the ramekins on the trivet. Cover the pot and cook on High for 13 minutes. Cool in the refrigerator and serve.

Lava Cake
Cook time: 20 minutes |Serves: 8| Per serving: Calories 208; Carbs 42g; Fat 4g; Protein 3g

Ingredients:

- 1 cup of all-purpose flour
- 1 cup of packed brown sugar, divided
- 5 tbsps. of baking cocoa, divided
- 2 tsps. of baking powder
- ¼ tsp. salt
- ½ cup milk
- 2 tbsps. oil
- ½ tsp. vanilla extract
- ⅛ tsp. ground cinnamon
- 1 ¼ cups of hot water

Directions:

In a bowl, whisk the flour, ½ cup of brown sugar, 3 tbsps. of cocoa, baking powder, and salt. In another bowl, whisk milk, oil, and vanilla. Add to flour mixture, stir just until moistened. Grease a baking dish and pour the batter in it. In a bowl, mix cinnamon and remaining ½ cup brown sugar and 2 tbsps. of cocoa. Stir in hot water and pour over the batter. Place a trivet and 1 cup of water in the pot. Cover the baking dish with foil and place it on the trivet. Cover the pot and cook on High for 20 minutes. Open, cool, and serve.

Peachy Cheesecake

Cook time: 30 minutes |Serves: 6| Per serving: Calories 262; Carbs 27g; Fat 12g; Protein 12g

Ingredients:

- 1 pkg. (8 oz.) reduced-fat cream cheese
- 4 oz. fat-free cream cheese
- ½ cup sugar
- ½ cup reduced-fat sour cream
- 2 tbsps. unsweetened apple juice
- 1 tbsp. all-purpose flour
- ½ tsp. vanilla
- 3 eggs, lightly beaten
- 2 medium ripe peaches, peeled and thinly sliced

Directions:

Place a trivet and 1 cup of water in the pot. Grease a springform pan. In a bowl, beat cream cheeses and sugar until smooth. Beat in sour cream, apple juice, flour, and vanilla. Add eggs and beat on low speed until just blended. Pour into the baking pan and cover the pan with foil. Place the baking pan on the trivet. Cover the pot and cook on High for 30 minutes. Open, cool, and serve.

Pear Dessert

Cook time: 15 minutes |Serves: 6| Per serving: Calories 180; Carbs 45g; Fat 1g; Protein 2g

Ingredients:

- 6 pears, peeled
- 1 bay leaf
- 4 cloves
- 1 cinnamon stick
- 1 tsp. ginger, grated
- 1 bottle red wine
- 2 cups of sugar
- 1 bunch of sage

Directions:

Put the wine in the pot. Add bay leaf, cloves, sugar, cinnamon, and ginger and mix well. Add pears, cover, and cook on High for 7 minutes. Open and transfer pears to plates. Heat the liquid on Sauté until it reduces. Drizzle the sauce over pears. Garnish with sage leaves and serve.

Apple Compote

Cook time: 5 minutes |Serves: 6| Per serving: Calories 150; Carbs 20g; Fat 2g; Protein 5g

Ingredients:

- 6 apples, cored and roughly chopped
- 8 tbsps. sugar
- 2 tsps. vanilla extract
- 3 drops lemon oil
- 3 drops mixed essential oil
- 1 and ½ tsp. cinnamon powder
- Water as needed

Directions:

Put apples in a bowl, cover with water. Add 3 drops of essential oil and leave aside for 10 minutes. Drain apples and transfer to the pot. Add lemon oil, sugar, vanilla extract, and cinnamon. Cover and cook on High for 5 minutes. Open and serve.

Poached Figs
Cook time: 4 minutes |Serves: 4| Per serving: Calories 140; Carbs 10g; Fat 3g; Protein 2g

Ingredients:

- 1 cup of red wine
- 1-pound of figs
- ½ cup of pine nuts
- Sugar to taste

Directions:

Put the wine and sugar in the pot. Mix and place the figs. Cover and cook on High for 4 minutes. Open and sprinkle with pine nuts. Serve.

Raspberry Curd
Cook time: 2 minutes |Serves: 4| Per serving: Calories 150; Carbs 12g; Fat 3g; Protein 3g

Ingredients:

- 2 tbsps. lemon juice
- 2 tbsps. oil
- Sugar to taste
- 12 ounces raspberries
- 2 tbsps. flax meal mixed with 4 tbsps. water

Directions:

Add everything in the pot and mix until sugar dissolves. Cover and cook on High. Serve.

Rice and Maple Syrup Pudding
Cook time: 20 minutes |Serves: 4 | Per serving: Calories 243; Carbs 18g; Fat 4g; Protein 13g

Ingredients:

- 1 cup brown rice
- ½ cup coconut chips
- 1 cup milk
- 4 tbsps. almonds
- 2 cups of water
- ½ cup maple syrup
- ¼ tsp. cinnamon powder
- 1 tbsp. raisins

Directions:

Put the rice, and water in the pot and cover. Cook on High for 15 minutes. Open and drain water. Add milk, chips, almonds, raisins, salt, cinnamon, and syrup. Mix and cover. Cook on High for 5 minutes. Serve.

Pineapple and Coconut Pudding

Cook time: 5 minutes |Serves: 8| Per serving: Calories 212; Carbs 17g; Fat 4g; Protein 5g

Ingredients:

- 1 tbsp. coconut oil
- 1 and ½ cups of water
- 1 cup whole rice
- 14 ounces of coconut milk
- 2 tbsps. of flax meal mixed with 3 tbsps. of water
- Stevia to the taste
- ½ tsp. vanilla extract
- 8 ounces canned pineapple, chopped

Directions:

In the pot, mix oil, water, and rice. Cover and cook on High for 3 minutes. Add stevia, milk, vanilla, flax meal, and pineapple. Stir and cover. Cook on High for 2 minutes. Serve.

Conclusion

The vegetarian diet is healthy. However, the diet can become dull if you do not have variety. This vegetarian Instant Pot cookbook offers hundreds of delicious recipes that are easy to cook. This book is great for both kitchen novices and seasoned home cooks who want to give the vegetarian diet a try. By following this guide, you will be able to make different types of meals every day so that you will not become bored while following this diet. This complete vegetarian Instant Pot cookbook gives you mouthwatering recipes that your entire family will enjoy, including meat-eaters.

Printed in Great Britain
by Amazon